Portrait of the Artist as Hermes

UNC | COLLEGE OF ARTS AND SCIENCES
Germanic and Slavic Languages and Literatures

From 1949 to 2004, UNC Press and the UNC Department of Germanic & Slavic Languages and Literatures published the UNC Studies in the Germanic Languages and Literatures series. Monographs, anthologies, and critical editions in the series covered an array of topics including medieval and modern literature, theater, linguistics, philology, onomastics, and the history of ideas. Through the generous support of the National Endowment for the Humanities and the Andrew W. Mellon Foundation, books in the series have been reissued in new paperback and open access digital editions. For a complete list of books visit www.uncpress.org.

Portrait of the Artist as Hermes

A Study of Myth and Psychology in Thomas Mann's *Felix Krull*

DONALD F. NELSON

UNC Studies in the Germanic Languages and Literatures
Number 70

Copyright © 1971

This work is licensed under a Creative Commons CC BY-NC-ND license. To view a copy of the license, visit http://creativecommons.org/licenses.

Suggested citation: Nelson, Donald F. *Portrait of the Artist as Hermes: A Study of Myth and Psychology in Thomas Mann's Felix Krull.* Chapel Hill: University of North Carolina Press, 1971. DOI: https://doi.org/10.5149/9781469658056_Nelson

Library of Congress Cataloging-in-Publication Data
Names: Nelson, Donald F.
Title: Portrait of the artist as Hermes : A study of myth and psychology in Thomas Mann's Felix Krull / by Donald F. Nelson.
Other titles: University of North Carolina Studies in the Germanic Languages and Literatures ; no. 70.
Description: Chapel Hill : University of North Carolina Press, [1971] Series: University of North Carolina Studies in the Germanic Languages and Literatures. | Includes bibliographical references.
Identifiers: LCCN 78030592 | ISBN 978-1-4696-5804-9 (pbk: alk. paper) | ISBN 978-1-4696-5805-6 (ebook)
Subjects: Mann, Thomas, 1875-1955. | Bekenntnisse des Hochstaplers Felix Krull.
Classification: LCC PT2625 .A44 B38 | DCC 833/ .912

For Barbara

PREFACE

Thomas Mann's novel, *The Confessions of Felix Krull*, contains a wealth of symbolic meaning on both a mythic and a psychoanalytical level. The impetus to the present study was the discovery that the key to this symbolism may be found in Jungian archetypal psychology and in Karl Kerenyi's studies on Hermes and on the archetypal image of mother and daughter. The fact that Mann explicitly and enthusiastically welcomed the collaboration of myth and psychology in the joint studies of Kerenyi and Jung and was also familiar with these studies led me to investigate the influence of their ideas on his novel. It soon became apparent that there was more than just a tenuous connection. Krull's character development and experiences showed a remarkable conformity not only to archetypal patterns associated with Hermes but also to Jung's theories of archetypal images and to his interpretations of Hermetic philosophy in medieval alchemy. The correspondences were so striking that it seemed most unlikely that they could have arisen by mere coincidence. My conclusion was that Mann had consciously utilized the core of Jung's and Kerenyi's archetypal theories and that *Felix Krull* could, in short, be read both as the story of a mythic identification with Hermes and of an odyssey into the archaic depths of the Jungian Collective Unconscious.

In this study Felix Krull is seen not as identical, but rather as *identifiable*, with Hermes. The extent to which these identifications are suggested by character and motif is the controlling idea of this book. The counterpart to this thematic line of investigation is presented in the concluding chapter in the form of stylistic analyses of select passages which aim at pointing out significant correspondences between style and subject. There I will attempt to show how the term "dialectic" best sums up the consistency of Mann's use of language and the organic interrelatedness of style and theme.

The mythopoeic and psychoanalytical critical perspectives are used in this book both alternately and in combination. While the theories of Jung and Kerenyi form the axis in terms of supporting evidence, I have not been averse to utilizing insights from Freudian psychology in my interpretation. It is not a question here of Freud versus Jung or "scientific psychoanalysis" versus "obscure mysticism." Rather, it is a matter ultimately of which of the two systems can provide the better explanation for a given phenomenon in Mann's work of literature. If, however, in the present study the Jungian interpretation prevails, it is only because I think Mann's novel can be better fitted into the Jungian system and its archetypal symbolism.

I have added to my knowledge of Hermes by drawing on a number of sources, the most rewarding of which were Walter F. Otto, *The Homeric Gods* (trans. Moses Hadas), Karl Kerenyi, *Hermes der Seelenführer*, and Norman O. Brown, *Hermes the Thief*. Since there is manifestly good reason to believe that it was Kerenyi who played the most influential role in reawakening Thomas Mann to the significance of Hermes, I regard his work as possessing the most immediate relevance to Mann's particular conception and representation of the Hermes-motif in *Felix Krull*. It will become apparent in the later chapters of this book that I have benefited greatly also from the work of Erich Neumann, especially his *Origins and History of Consciousness* (trans. R. F. C. Hull) and *The Great Mother* (trans. Ralph Manheim).

All quotations from Mann's works are from *Gesammelte Werke in zwölf Bänden* (S. Fischer Verlag, 1960). Quotations from *Bekenntnisse des Hochstaplers Felix Krull* are from Volume Seven of this edition. All translations of passages from Mann are my own. In these instances I must take the sole responsibility for any egregious unwieldiness of the English. From such secondary sources as Jung, Neumann, and Otto I have preferred to quote exclusively from the English translations to avoid having the appearance of the text proper dwarfed through copious translations in the footnotes.

DONALD F. NELSON

Columbus, Ohio
September 1970

ACKNOWLEDGMENTS

I am very grateful to my colleagues Oskar Seidlin and Hugo Bekker who read the manuscript and offered valuable criticism and encouragement without necessarily endorsing or approving of everything in it. To Professor Robert Lenardon of the Department of Classics at Ohio State University I owe thanks for his generous assistance in interpreting passages in Latin pertaining to Hermes and for furnishing me with textual material along with his critical comments.

This book was supported, in part, by the Ohio State University Development Fund through its Faculty Summer Fellowship in the Humanities, 1969.

Grateful acknowledgment is hereby made to the following publishers for permission to quote from the works indicated:
S. Fischer Verlag: Thomas Mann, *Gesammelte Werke in zwölf Bänden* (1960).
The Macmillan Company: J. G. Frazer: *The Golden Bough* (1922).
Pantheon Books Inc.: Walter F. Otto, *The Homeric Gods*, trans. Moses Hadas (1954).
Rhein-Verlag: Karl Kerenyi, *Romandichtung und Mythologie* (1945).

Finally, I should like to express my gratitude to Arliss Roaden, Dean of the Graduate School of Ohio State University, for aiding the publication of this book with a grant from the Graduate School.

CONTENTS

I	INTRODUCTION	1
II	BEYOND GOOD AND EVIL	12
III	HERMAPHRODITUS AND THE PRIMAL HERMES	21
IV	DIVINE ANDROGYNY AND SELF-SUFFICIENT NARCISSISM	29
V	DIANA THE PROVIDER	45
VI	THE ELEUSINIAN MYSTERIES REVISITED	57
VII	MERCURIUS, ALCHEMY, AND THE UNION OF OPPOSITES	99
VIII	THE DIALECTIC OF THE HERMETIC STYLE	107
	NOTES	129
	SELECTED BIBLIOGRAPHY	143
	GENERAL INDEX	146

I. INTRODUCTION

With its genesis encompassing a period of nearly fifty years, *Felix Krull*, published in 1954, constitutes in a sense Thomas Mann's life work. It is a rich orchestration and recapitulation of the author's most personal and urgent themes, though these often appear, to be sure, in the most unexpected and frivolous guises. Like the titular hero, the identity of the work – with respect to genre-classification – is protean and iridescent, resisting categorical definition. The work is plurisignificant and admits of identifications with a multiplicity of themes and forms of past traditions. It is certainly, on one level, a novel of picaresque adventure in the manner of Grimmelshausen's *Simplicissimus* with regard to plot and subject[1]; and in terms of style it is clearly a parody of confessional memoir in the tradition of Saint Augustine, Rousseau, and Goethe. It is also possible to view Krull's development as the ironic reversal of the traditional *Bildungsroman* epitomized in Germany by Goethe's *Wilhelm Meister*.[2] While on the one hand there is no quarrel about the validity of these interpretations, there is, on the other hand, some question as to their inclusiveness in view of the distinctly mythic dimension which the work takes on in the later stages of its development. It is, therefore, not my purpose to offer a mythic-psychoanalytical perspective as a substitute or even as an alternative to previous interpretations of *Felix Krull*. Instead, I prefer to view my approach as necessarily complementary, for Krull fits equally well into the roles of picaresque rogue and Hermes – these being by no means mutually exclusive.

It is, in fact, the Hermes-motif which is the most distinctly identifiable mythic aspect of *Felix Krull*. A number of studies have made cursory reference to this motif both in the Joseph-stories and in *Felix Krull*, but the sum of these references amounts to either a series of disconnected particulars or of unelaborated generalities. The studies, in which a concern with the motif is central rather than incidental, limit themselves, for the most part, to cataloguing a number of Hermes-epithets embodied in Joseph and Felix Krull. The differences in their merit have therefore been largely quantitative.[3] From a mythopoeic critical perspective, a catalogue of Hermes-epithets, no matter how complete, remains essentially at the level of character analysis and description. What is lacking is the larger mythic perspective, specifically, a frame of reference in which the character epithets are integrated with plot and interrelated, in turn, to universal mythic patterns of behavior and experience. In the present study the analysis goes beyond an identification with a mythic personage to a more detailed consideration of plot and an identification with recurrent mythic patterns and archetypal experiences extrapolated from the novel's system of symbols.

The Thomas Mann studies which have transcended the descriptive level of mythological

INTRODUCTION

identification are, in my opinion, those which draw on psychoanalytic insights in interpreting myth.[4] In applying psychoanalysis to mythology and anthropology, Freud and Jung strove to penetrate to the primary origins of behavior and experience. This necessitated the assumption of a collective unconscious as the ultimate source of universality of psychic experience.[5] The groundwork for their theories had been prepared by the nineteenth-century anthropological Darwinists in whose writings we find the idea of cultural universals.[6] Adolf Bastian, E. B. Tylor, and J. G. Frazer recognized and stressed the constancy of certain elementary ideas in mankind which cut across cultural boundaries. The importance of Freud and Jung in this context is that their work went beyond the anthropologists' cataloguing and description of these universals and the theories of cultural diffusion to account for them to a study of their psychobiological roots.

The legitimization for applying a mythopoeic and psychoanalytic approach to the later work of Thomas Mann is given by Mann himself. His most explicit statements on the relation of psychoanalysis to myth and the interaction of these with creative literature are to be found in the essay "Freud und die Zukunft" ("Freud and the Future"), written in 1936. "Das mythische Interesse," Mann says, "ist der Psychoanalyse genau so eingeboren, wie allem Dichtertum das psychologische Interesse eingeboren ist. Ihr Zurückdringen in die Kindheit der Einzelseele ist zugleich auch schon das Zurückdringen in die Kindheit des Menschen, ins Primitive und in die Mythik." (IX, 492)* Although this essay on Freud was written during the period of work on the Joseph cycle and many of the remarks on the collective unconscious and the identification with a mythic prototype are made with specific reference to the Joseph-stories, it should not be inferred from this that Mann's interest in myth and psychoanalysis waned in subsequent years. The correspondence with Kerenyi, the presence of the Hermes-motif in *Felix Krull*, and the kinship in character between Joseph and Felix Krull attest to the fact that the interest remained very much alive; it is testimony of Mann's creative continuity.

Nevertheless, such a felicitous legitimization of method does not preclude basic misconceptions concerning the implications of a mythopoeic and and psychoanalytic approach to literature. A frequent criticism is that these approaches tend to be unduly reductive in the sense that, by stressing the typical nature of behavior and experience, they deprive fictional characters of their individuality. Within the framework of psychoanalysis, however, individuality is never absolute, but relative. Despite their basic disagreements, both

---

* "The interest in myth is just as native to psychoanalysis as the interest in psychology is to all creative literature. Its penetration into the childhood of the individual soul is also a penetration into the childhood of mankind, into the primitive and mythic."

INTRODUCTION

Freudian and Jungian psychology assume that in the unconscious mankind has a common psychological character analogous to universal patterns of biological and instinctual behavior. Accordingly, what is individual in human behavior tends to be more of a surface phenomenon, a factor connected with ego consciousness.[7] The universal and ahistorical nature of a considerable part of behavior and experience is more latent than overt in man.

This psychoanalytical insight into the relativity of individuality and the mingling of the individual and the typical informs the underlying aesthetic of the Joseph cycle, as Thomas Mann himself admits in the essay on Freud. Here, Mann cites an article, "Zur Psychologie älterer Biographik," by a psychoanalyst of the Freudian school, Ernst Kris.[8] For Mann, the chief implication of this article is that many persons live not an individual life but a biographical type. "Die Frage jener Schrift," Mann asserts, "geht nun aber dahin, ob sich denn die Grenze zwischen dem, was Formelgut legendärer Biographik, und dem, was Lebenseigentum des Künstlers ist, zwischen dem Typischen und dem Individuellen also, scharf und unzweideutig ziehen lasse..." (IX,492)* The question, Mann says, is negated by its very for-

* "The question raised by the article is whether a line of demarcation can be sharply and unequivocally drawn between the formal stock-in-trade of legendary biography and the life of the individual artist – in other words, between the typical and the individual?"

mulation. "Das Leben ist tatsächlich eine Mischung von formelhaften und individuellen Elementen, ein Ineinander, bei dem das Individuelle gleichsam nur über das Formelhaft-Unpersönliche hinausragt." (IX,492)* Mann concludes that the typical is actually the mythical, that one might just as well say "lived myth" as "lived life." He goes on to point out that "der gelebte Mythus" ("the myth as lived") is the epic idea embodied in his Joseph novel. According to this idea, the supposed "individual" naïvely believes himself to be unique and is unaware of the extent to which his life is but a formula and a repetition and his path is already marked out for him by those who trod it before him.

In connection with the relativity of individuality it is necessary to obviate a second misunderstanding, at the bottom of which lies a confusion between homology and analogy. In stressing the identification of characters and plot with a mythic prototype, it makes a difference whether we talk about them as being homologous (i.e., similar) in structure to the prototype or whether we instead stress that they are analogous in function to the prototype.[9] According to this distinction, a mythopoeic interpretation may be more fruitful if it recognizes, especially with respect to plot, similarity of function as more significant than homology

---

* "Life is actually a mingling of the formal stock-in-trade and the individual elements, a fusion in which the individual, as it were, just manages to raise his head above the formal and impersonal elements."

INTRODUCTION

of structure or content. In addition to the relativity of individuality it is thus necessary to postulate here the relativity of identicalness. Literary personages and plots are never carbon copies of mythic prototypes. Whenever, in the present study, mention is made of significant parallels to mythic patterns, the analogous, rather than the homologous, nature of character, experience, and plot is stressed. Just as a symbol is never identical with its referent, so also can a character or the character's experience never be completely equated with a prototype. To expect a point-for-point correspondence between character and mythic personage and between plot and mythic pattern is to misconstrue both the author's aesthetic and the underlying principle of the mythopoeic approach employed in this study which is essentially the re-creative possibilities inherent in analogical thinking. While it is true that the number of mythic personages and archetypal experiences is infinite and that many mythological figures possess within themselves antithetical character traits, it does not follow from this that almost any identification of literary figure and mythological prototype is possible. An analogy between the grammar of a language and mythic pattern may serve to illustrate this point. Both are characterized by the existence of certain empirical constraints on the indiscriminate manipulation or ordering of their elements. In any language the number of possible grammatically correct utterances is infinite. Yet a native speaker of English, for example, whose competence in the language exceeds that of a small child, can readily discern an ungrammatical utterance such as: *Come has he not yet. The process involved here is one of recognition. Linguistic competence enables us to recognize that the utterance does not conform to accepted patterns. In the same way, it may be said, mythology is characterized by a virtually infinite number of patterns with respect to character and plot. Yet the scholar who has achieved a fair degree of competence in the areas of mythology and comparative religion may recognize elements that do not conform to mythic pattern. For example, ugliness of physical stature and clumsiness do not fit the mythic pattern of Hermes' character by any stretch of the imagination. There is no possible way, furthermore, of constructing an argument which would permit us to identify Felix Krull with Apollo rather than with Hermes. It is, ultimately, always a question of whether a motif fits into a pattern or not. The recognition that a motif fits organically into the pattern of the universe of a literary work and does not violate the basic principles of analogy is vital to the re-creative experience of reader and critic alike in dealing with a work of literature.

Finally, the mythopoeic critic must address himself to the question whether the artist consciously used myth as a basis for his work. In the case of Thomas Mann, it is obvious that he utilized mythic and psychoanalytical ideas in the creation of the Joseph cycle. But in the absence of other

INTRODUCTION

specific documentary evidence it becomes a matter of speculation in determining whether the author was familiar with a specific myth or mythic personage or their numerous variants. If, however, one is able to discern meaningful, coherent, and illuminating parallels between character and mythic prototype or between plot and mythic pattern, then one should feel justified in interpreting the particular aspect of the work in terms of a particular myth, especially if the myth provides a framework within which characters, experiences, and plot assume a greater coherence of meaning and organic interrelationship.[10] In adopting this criterion, one is able to show that some episodes which appear fragmentary or disconnected are actually complete and integrally related to the whole through the myth. This criterion amounts to more than what is traditionally referred to as "common sense." It is, to be sure, a matter of making sense out of something that otherwise might appear extraneous or nonsensical, but beyond that it is also a matter of whether the interpretation is congruent within the universe which the artist has created in his work. Again, just as a competent speaker of a language is able, through knowledge of the grammar of that language, to discern whether a novel utterance conforms to established patterns within the universe of that grammar, so also should it be possible, through internalization of an artist's "grammar," to intuit whether a new element conforms to established patterns within the universe of his work.

INTRODUCTION

In the present study of *Felix Krull*, I have had to make a number of speculative assumptions concerning Mann's use of myth and psychoanalysis which may appear much less permissible than in a treatment of the Joseph-stories; for Mann's essays and letters contain no explicit references as to the extent to which this last of his novels is informed with mythic and psychoanalytic ideas. The basis and starting point for subsequent assumptions that underlie my interpretation are the explicit references in the work itself which permit an identification of Krull with Hermes and suggest also a kinship in character between Krull and Joseph. This establishes the basis for a mythic interpretation. Both Joseph and Krull have in common characteristics of androgyny and narcissism, which suggests Mann's indebtedness to Jung and Freud respectively. The parallels between Joseph and Krull in character and development extend, of course, much further than this. The fact that both, at first, have the naïve belief that they are uniquely individual only to discover later that their existences conform to a prototype indicates that Mann has informed *Felix Krull* with essentially the same mythic and psychological principles discussed in "Freud and the Future," although these are decidedly more latent in *Felix Krull*. I assume, furthermore, that Mann's familiarity with the interpretation of myth along the lines of Jungian archetypal psychology was intensified at the stimulus of Karl Kerenyi. The published correspondence,

Romandichtung und Mythologie, offers valuable hints which support this assumption. Here Mann states his enthusiastic approval of the collaboration between Jung and Kerenyi and gives testimony of his growing preoccupation with Hermes.[11] The letters to Kerenyi suggest, in sum, a deepening and broadening of Mann's mythic perspective in addition to a greater familiarity with the literature in the field.[12] It is reasonable to assume, therefore, that this enrichment of knowledge benefited his subsequent creations, not least of all *Felix Krull.*

II. BEYOND GOOD AND EVIL

Karl Kerenyi begins his book, *Hermes der Seelenführer*, by asking two interrelated questions, first, what the ancient Greek image of Hermes was, and second, how this image could be associated with a divinity. The latter question is somewhat more intriguing than the first because of the insinuation that lurks behind it. For Hermes encompasses within the totality of his being some very dubious traits of character. For example: how are we to reconcile the incongruity in the fact that although Hermes safely guides lonely and unprotected wayfarers past highway robbers, he is at the same time the patron of the menacing thief with whom he even has an affinity and bond of affection? A provisional answer might be that the contradiction is actually not reconcilable, but that it may be resolved once we realize that throughout man's religious history divinities have not only elicited ambivalence but have also enjoyed the privilege of being beyond good and evil. As for Hermes the cunning trickster and thief, surely such an astonishingly precocious feat as his theft – on the very day he was born – of Apollo's cattle was one of his many master strokes that elicited wonderment among mortals and entitled him to the status of a superhuman being. In *The Golden Bough* Frazer points out that in the transition from magic to religion there is the widespread belief that "the gods themselves are adepts in magic, guarding their persons by talismans and working their will by spells and incantations."[1] Norman Brown argues that the ancient image of Hermes is most intelligible if we see its evolution as proceeding from Hermes the Magician to Hermes the Trickster to Hermes the Thief.[2] Hermes' trickery and success at theft are generally represented as a "manifestation of magical power."[3] In Brown's view, trickery and magic are so intimately related in primitive thought that the mind makes no clear distinction between them, and in the Homeric period, in turn, philological analysis indicates that there is no clearcut semantic distinction between "theft" and "trickery."[4] All of this suggests, then, that to the preclassical Greek mind Hermes was preeminently a magician with secret powers and that the particular use to which he put these powers was a matter of secondary importance.

Kerenyi's question may be reshaped and applied to Thomas Mann: how was Mann able to associate Felix Krull with Hermes? The answer is already partially suggested by the motifs that have cropped up in the foregoing analysis. I shall first elaborate on these connections and then go on to trace further parallels. All of this will be in the form of a preliminary sketch, and many of the points touched on constitute only minor motifs. The major motifs will be taken up and developed more fully in the ensuing chapters.

It is to be noted, first of all, that the actual association of Krull with Hermes does not take place until the later part of the work. It is Madame Houpflé, alias Diane Philibert, who makes the identification, referring in awed contemplation of Krull's statuesque nakedness to his "Hermes legs." When Krull confesses that he stole her jewels, she proclaims to her impassioned amusement that he does not know who Hermes is and yet *is* Hermes himself. To complete the ritual, she phonetically associates and blends the name Armand with the French form Hermès. It is Krull's theft of Madame Houpflé's jewels, then, which affords the concrete basis for his identification with Hermes the thief. In fact, the manner in which the theft is executed reveals a significant parallel to Hermes' character. At the Straßburg customs inspection Krull tries to make us believe that the precious jewel case "slipped" mysteriously and unawares into his own bag, "as if chance had so decreed it." Norman Brown points out that in Greek the characteristic epithets applied to Hermes the Thief are derivatives of the verb *kleptein* (cf. the English derivative *cleptomaniac*) which, in Homeric Greek, did not yet mean "to steal," but rather "to remove secretly" and, more frequently, "to deceive."[5] This suggests that the original meaning of the root was "secret action." In English the word that most closely corresponds to this core of meaning is "stealth" which does not clearly distinguish between "stealing" and "secret action." The degree to which this spread of meaning coincides with the nature of Krull's act is remarkable. Surely the reader does not take Krull's specious reasoning at face value. As far as we are concerned, it is theft, but theft of a very "secret" or "stealthy" kind. Thus both Krull and Hermes are characterized by "stealth" in all its ambiguity of meaning.

Related to stealth are cunning and trickery. These involve not only stealthy activity but also the art of sly calculation and guile in verbal exchange. In the Homeric Hymn we learn that after he had been called to account by Apollo for the theft of his cattle, Hermes displayed extraordinary shrewdness in repartee and bargaining. In the pawnshop episode Krull proves himself to be a smooth talker, "stealthy" in the use of words and shrewd in bargaining, though it appears that the watchmaker, Master Jean-Pierre, is a tougher opponent for him than Apollo was for Hermes. Krull's deftness of verbal exchange and repartee is one of his outstanding traits, and it elicits praise from Jean-Pierre who notes that along with his other talents he also has a glib tongue.

Like the mythological gods, Krull's character embraces contradictions which render his total personality dualistic and ambivalent. In contrast to his need of remaining coolly aloof from the bourgeois social world and the vulgarity of its behavior patterns, he is yet friendly and kind in most of his encounters with persons of both humble and elevated status. Hermes, it is generally agreed, was of all gods the friendliest toward mankind, although this amiability extended to elements which undermined the security and welfare of society. Though both Krull and Hermes are tricksters, their trickery, ironically, never seems to bring harm. On the contrary, it appears to be the source of joy and happiness to humans. Madame Houpflé is positively exhilarated upon learning that it was Krull who stole her jewels, to which he replies that he knew that it would give her pleasure. In the Homeric age, Hermes' trickery is also related to technical skill which brings benefits to humanity and promotes human welfare.[6] Two of his epithets in this connection are "giver of good things" and "giver of joy." To the modern consciousness the identity of trickster and cultural hero may seem delightfully ironic, but in preclassical Greece it appears to have been a solemn association. One of Krull's traits which is related to trickery and virtuosity – his glibness and comical, parodistic mode of speech – often gives rise to both amusement and vexation in those with whom he comes in contact. Not only his verbal behavior, but his physical appearance also incites ambivalent responses. This ambivalence is indeed a dominant theme about which more will be said later.

It was pointed out that Hermes the Trickster derives from Hermes the Magician, since the pre-logical mind sees trickery as a manifestation of magical power. One of Hermes' more baffling traits is that he is suddenly and magically present when least expected.[7] We are reminded of the episode in which Marquis de Venosta is astonished by the totally unexpected presence of Krull as guest and man of distinction in a fashionable hotel restaurant frequented by exclusive clientele.

This leads to a very witty and profoundly meaningful exchange of words concerning Krull's status. Krull's activities as waiter and distinguished gentleman "go on concurrently." He is both "here and there," to which Venosta replies: "Très amusant. Sie sind ein Zauberer" ("You are a magician"). We might relate this to W. F. Otto's statement concerning Hermes the traveler: "It is in his nature not to belong to any locality and not to possess any permanent abode; always he is on the road between here and yonder, and suddenly he joins some solitary wayfarer."[8] Krull's ability to assume various roles and to perform multifarious feats might be associated on a mythological plane with secret and magic powers. In fact, the word "geheim" ("secret") is repeatedly used in describing these feats. He is eminently successful in his impersonations, as an illusionist, and in the performance of whatever requires manual skill and adroitness, whether it be running an elevator, serving dishes, playing a violin, or tennis. The early Greeks interpreted success at craftmanship as the possession of magical powers. Essentially, primitive magic aimed at the manipulation of the external world. Krull's feigning of an epileptic seizure to avoid military draft is an eminent example of manipulating the external world to one's own ends. Because of his adroitness and technical skills of a sort, Krull, like Hermes, may be called a craftsman and virtuoso. His skill as a waiter has its counterpart in Hermes the patron of servants. Hermes possessed all the qualities which enabled him to become servant to the Olympians – skill in lighting the fire, splitting kindling wood, roasting and carving meat, and pouring wine.[9] In Attic drama and in the *Odyssey* his "role" is that of servant and messenger to Zeus, and in Alcaeus and Sappho he is cupbearer to the gods.[10] He is, in effect, a herald whose office combines a great diversity of functions ranging from the king's personal cook to an agent of international negotiations in which his ministry is based on the craft of knowing the ceremonial proprieties. Krull's success in various forms of hotel service qualifies him as the peer of Hermes in adroitness. Need I remind the reader that later, as Marquis de Venosta, Krull excels in a form of ministerial function at the court of Dom Carlos? Although, in the estimation of Venosta's mother, he may have overstepped the bounds of ceremonial propriety in relating the anecdote about the temporary lapse in housebrokenness on the part of the family dog, this is not an indication of ignorance as to propriety, but an expression of the liberating force of the imagination in the service of entertaining and giving joy to a king. The gaiety at the court unleashed by this anecdote exonerates Krull from the charge of a *faux pas*.

The thief, cunning trickster, magician, skillful craftsman, adroit servant, ceremonial minister, the giver of joy, the smooth talker and shrewd negotiator – these are the traits that Krull shares with Hermes. We may speak here of a mythical identification in the sense that Krull re-enacts in strikingly parallel capacities the career of his mythical prototype. The basis for the identification seems inherent in Krull from the beginning, but remains submerged below the threshold of consciousness until it is brought to awareness by Diane Philibert. The identification, therefore, does not come in any way unprepared. From the very beginning Krull is aware that he is an extraordinary and elect personality, "favored by heaven" and in possession of special atrributes which elevate him to a godlike stature. His experience with Diane Philibert is but the ultimate confirmation of his divination.

With all the character parallels between Krull and Hermes, it is interesting that there is one outstanding trait of the Greek divinity that appears to be absent in Mann's protagonist – Hermes *psychopompos* or conductor of the departed souls to Hades. It was in this capacity that Hermes had made his initial appearance in Mann's work in *Death in Venice*, guiding Aschenbach's soul on its journey to the Underworld. *Felix Krull* is a novel about life, not death. Yet, it is possible to see an association with guiding souls both upward and downward in Krull's function as elevator operator. It is not by accident that he is given the name Armand – with its phonetic proximity to the French Hermès – precisely on the day before assuming this duty. The fact that he is given the name of the previous elevator boy makes him a "successor."

The emergence of identifiable mythic associations and motifs in the later part of the *Confessions* derives from the fact that Mann's interest in the mythical and his awareness of the significance of Hermes for his literary work was a late development. At the same time, one cannot help but ponder over the amazing and curious circumstance that the early development of Felix Krull appears to be an unconscious prefiguration of his role as Hermes. I do not believe we can dismiss the possibility that the idea of Hermes did figure in Mann's original conception of the work.[11] An association with Hermes in the portrait of the early Felix Krull, however vague and dimly conscious it may have been, is plausible owing to the presence of the Hermes-motif in *Death in Venice* and *The Magic Mountain*. In the absence of documentary evidence, however, all of this must remain in the realm of speculation. Furthermore, it is probable that Mann's early knowledge about Hermes did not extend beyond conventional wisdom. At best, it can be said that the Hermes-motif is powerfully latent in the early fragment of the *Confessions* only to become overt and significantly functional with Mann's changing conception and heightened awareness of the significance of the mythical and the archetypal during his preparatory studies for the Joseph novels.

III. HERMAPHRODITUS AND THE PRIMAL HERMES

In the Fourth Book of Ovid's *Metamorphoses* we are told that the nymph Salmacis fell in love with the youth Hermaphroditus, the son of Hermes and Aphrodite, who tenaciously resisted her advances. While he was bathing, she plunged into the water, clasped the reluctant god in her arms, entwined herself around him like ivy around the trunk of a tree with the result that the two became unicorporally merged. The narrator, the nymph Alcithoe, relates that they seemed to have no sex, and yet to have both. Ovid's account is apparently designed to give an explanation of the genesis of the bisexual figure which plays a prominent role in ancient ritual and art. But the origin as well as the nature of Hermaphrodite seem hopelessly obscure owing to the many conflicting versions.[1] Most Greek legends, for example, see Hermaphrodite as the product of birth, of the union of Hermes and Aphrodite, and not, like Ovid, as the result of a metamorphosis. However numerous and contradictory the variants concerning the origin of the hermaphrodite figure may be, the interesting fact is that Hermes and Aphrodite are frequently associated with one another in ritual and that both are somehow linked with the figure of Hermaphroditus, a bisexual being which was worshipped and celebrated in popular cults as a symbol in which the polarity of the sexes is resolved and brought back to a state of primordial unity.

In his book, *Hermes der Seelenführer*, Karl Kerenyi gives an interpretation of the connection between Hermes and the bisexual god which, I believe, influenced Mann's later conception of *Felix Krull*.[2] Kerenyi infers that Hermes and Aphrodite were originally two aspects of the same primal being.[3] As an object of ritual worship, the hermaphrodite figure is a primitive, pre-Olympian type of divine image and is found in the cult of Hermes and Aphrodite in Argos and in the Cyprian cult of Aphroditos. In the latter, the bisexual figure is represented as the male aspect of Aphrodite and is clad as a woman. It is possible, Kerenyi infers, to identify this Aphroditos as the primal Hermes himself.[4] This suggests that the primal Hermes was hermaphroditic, of indeterminate sex.[5] Kerenyi links this ambiguous sexuality with an urmythological theme of great significance – the initial evocation and individuation of the male principle through the female.

I believe that this interpretation of the primal Hermes as hermaphroditic and the theme of the ultimate ascendancy of the male principle as the dominant aspect of Hermes' being provided Mann with a novel insight to be exploited for literary purposes. By tracing significant parallels I hope to demonstrate that in the *Confessions* there are refractions of this germinal motif in Felix Krull's character and development. Owing to the frequent comic twists and reversals occasioned by Mann's parodistic treatment of models these parallels exhibit varying degrees of conformity to the archetypal patterns and motifs. The merit of such an interpretation, if it is valid, is that it brings out a greater coherence and more intelligible continuity between such key episodes and motifs as the balcony scene with the brother-sister pair, Krull's ambivalent nature and his androgynous character, his narcissism, the affair with Diane Philibert, his "worship" of Andromache, and his experience with the mother-daughter pair in Zouzou and Senhora Kuckuck. All of these are closely interrelated, and each will be treated in its proper sequence. For the present, it will be necessary to deal with the particulars of Kerenyi's account of the evocation of the male principle;[6] the proper understanding of this theory is an important prerequisite for the intelligibility of my development of theme.

Kerenyi cites a genealogical account given by Cicero which contains conflicting versions concerning the identity of the goddess with whom Hermes consorted to beget Eros. According to one source it was Artemis (Diana), while another mythologem identifies her as Aphrodite[7]. Both versions, Kerenyi argues, may be reconciled by condensing them into a single urmyth which has as its main theme the initial evocation or the distinctly male principle through the female. Kerenyi's deduction is based on the above-mentioned inference that the primal Hermes was part of an hermaphroditic figure or image with Aphrodite as his female counterpart. This primal Hermes, then, is not an unequivocally male being. Furthermore, Aphrodite, in this pre-Olympian mythologem, is Hermes' sister, both having descended from Uranos (Heaven) and Hemera (Day). Thus, it was not necessary, according to Kerenyi, for Hermes to have a special union with Aphrodite in order to beget Eros, since she already constituted the female aspect of their hermaphroditic fusion. The bisexual divinity is self-fecundating. What is more, there is reason to believe that this female aspect was originally predominant in the fusion, the masculinity of Hermes remaining latent and subordinate until the male principle was fully aroused in him. As for the primal goddess, the great *evocatrice*, who was responsible for this arousal in the form of phallic excitation, Cicero mentions two names: Persephone (the daughter of Demeter), and Artemis, the same goddess who, according to the mythological variant already mentioned, is reported to have given birth to Eros out of the union with Hermes.[8] The Roman poet Propertius mentions a third name – Brimo.[9] The latter, according to Kerenyi, was originally united with Persephone and Artemis in a single tripartite figure.[10] We have here a prime example of the interchangeability of personages and identities in the fluid mythological world. Brimo, a goddess of northern Greece, was identifiable on the one hand with Demeter and Persephone – the mother-daughter pair whose identity or bi-unity formed the nucleus of the Eleusinian Mysteries – and with Artemis on the other, since she contained germinally all three in herself. In her elementary virginity, Brimo encounters the unawakened masculinity of Hermes which she arouses to a state of unequivocal phallic virility. This, by way of conjecture, must have also involved Hermes' separation from the bisexual fusion, though he never became completely dissociated from it, as attested by by the cult rituals in which Hermes and Aphrodite are repeatedly connected. That the two later gave birth, within the Olympian context, to Hermaphroditus might be explained as an instance of a mythical *repetitio* in which is symbolized the identity of father and son, of begetter and begotten. Thus the son, Hermaphroditus, repeats in modified version the bisexual existence of his father.

In this mythologem of the primal Hermes we are presented with a number of motifs which find expression in *Felix Krull* either in the form of refracted images or as adaptations in which striking parallels may be traced. There is first of all the association of Hermes with some form of bisexuality, whether it be hermaphroditism or androgyny. The original indeterminateness of his sex is refracted in Krull's peculiar form of physical attractiveness which, even by his own confession, gives his person a cast of sexual intermediateness – an extraordinary being in between – so that on occasion he stirs homosexual impulses in men, while at the same time remaining attractive to women. It is more appropriate to designate this aspect of Krull as androgynous rather than hermaphroditic, since the former denotes bisexuality in a more figurative sense, while the latter always stresses the concrete, anatomical bisexuality in terms of the reproductive organs, though to the Greek mind it was no less symbolic.

In the pre-Olympian myth, as we have noted, Aphrodite, who constitutes the female aspect of the hermaphrodite figure in which Hermes is the subordinate male counterpart, is none other than Hermes' sister. What is significant here is not so much the association with brother-sister incest, but rather the fact that the hermaphrodite figure consists of a brother-sister pair. Krull's attraction to pairs of persons, to which he consistently refers as the "double image," is initiated by the emergence of a brother-sister pair on the balcony of a Frankfurt hotel which excites his imagination by virtue of the idea of complementary unity that it evokes. Intimations of unity is a persistent theme in *Felix Krull*, and the brother-sister pair is the first important link in a chain of motifs having to do with complementaries and the idea of unity in duality.

The arousal of the male principle in Hermes to a status of dominance appears on first sight to have no discernible parallel in the development of Felix Krull. But we do not have to look far for an intimation of its oblique representation if we consider one of the female divinities mythologically connected with it – Artemis. Is it a mere coincidence that the person who first awakens in Krull his identity with Hermes has the name Diane which, in Roman mythology, is the name given to Artemis' counterpart? I think not, despite the fact that an attempt to establish parallels between the eccentric, middle-aged authoress and the youthful virgin Diana may seem utterly far-fetched and specious. The task here will be to present convincing evidence that Krull's affair with Diane Philibert, however burlesque it may appear, constitutes a turning point in his development, not only with respect to his new mythical identity but also in terms of his sexuality.

The mythological identity of Artemis and Persephone raises two questions. First, with which character in the novel are we to identify Persephone? And secondly, what, if any, is her relation ship to Diane Philibert, the refracted image of Artemis? Persephone, the virgin daughter of Demeter (the Great Goddess of the Earth and prototypical mother image) – who else but Zouzou, the daughter of Senhora Kuckuck, could better conform to the archetype? Not only does she arouse Krull's erotic feelings to the point where he is obsessed with the idea of seducing her, but she also constitutes, together with her mother, another fascinating "double image" which admits of identification with the mother-daughter pair, Demeter and Persephone, of the Eleusinian Mysteries. In the Demeter myth it is Hermes who is entrusted by Zeus with the mission of returning Persephone – who had been abducted by Pluto to Hades – from the underworld to her grieving mother. Mann appears to have dealt much more freely with this latter motif by giving it an ironic twist – Krull-Hermes appears here in the role of seducer rather than as trustworthy messenger and mediator. What links Artemis-Diane with Zouzou is the role they play as arousers of Krull's eroticism, though each contributes differently. Finally, it is the protean character of Krull – his own change of identities as well as his idea of the interchangeability of identities in the world surrounding him – that corresponds so fittingly to the nature of the mythological world. All these considerations establish the perspective for a mythopoeic interpretation of the work.

IV. DIVINE ANDROGYNY AND SELF-SUFFICIENT NARCISSISM

When Krull informs us that he posed nude for a legendary role from Greek mythology put to canvas by his Godfather Schimmelpreester, he attributes to himself a godlike stature: "... ich war überaus angenehm und göttergleich gewachsen, schlank, weich und doch kräftig von Gliedern, goldig von Haut und ohne Tadel in Hinsicht auf schönes Ebenmaß." (284)* The epithets in this description emphasize classical ideals of harmony and symmetry. They are also suggestive of another characteristic of classical Greek art, especially of fourth century works – its sexual dimorphism.[1] This trend seeks to bring out androgynous qualities in the representation of divinities. The aim of the sculptors of this period appears to be the realization of a synthesis in which the aesthetic virility of man and the graceful beauty of woman blend into one. Differences in both size and structure between the male and the female body are minimized. While the male sculptured figures exhibit small waists, prominent buttocks, and well-defined pectorals, the female figures display narrow hips, barely discernible waists and small breasts set wide apart. In addition, men are generally not represented as taller than women. All androgynous representation, in myth as in artistic creation, symbolizes the wholeness resulting from the fusion of the sexes, a union whereby each sex

* "My stature was extremely pleasing and godlike, slender, delicate and yet powerful in build, golden in skin, and flawless with respect to symmetry of proportion."

receives something of the powers of the other. It symbolizes both the state of primordial hermaphroditic unity of Man and the dream of a return to that unity.

Other descriptions of Krull's physiognomy and physique also contain subtle hints of androgyny: "Ich aber besaß seidenweiches Haar, wie man es nur selten beim männlichen Geschlechte findet..." (273)* "Mein Wuchs ... war keineswegs robust, an allen Gliedern und Muskeln jedoch so gleichmäßig-maßvoll entwickelt, wie es sonst nur bei Liebhabern des Sports ... zu sein pflegt... Ferner ist anzumerken, daß meine Haut von außerordentlich zarter Beschaffenheit... war..." (328)** This androgynous cast excites homosexual impulses in Monsieur Stürzli, the hotel owner. Krull understands perfectly well that this is a consequence of his youthful beauty in which "... die Grenze zwischen dem Sinnlichen in seiner allgemeinsten und in seiner engeren Bedeutung nicht so ganz leicht zu ziehen ist..." (411)*** There are also the cases of certain vagrant gentlemen, "Schwärmer, welche nicht die Frau suchen, aber

---

* "My hair was silken soft, as is seldom the case in the male sex."
** "My physique was by no means robust, yet every limb and every muscle was developed with an evenness of proportion usually found only in devotees of sports... I must further note that the texture of my skin was extraordinarily delicate."
*** "... the boundary between the sensual in its most general and in its more specific sense cannot be so easily drawn."

DIVINE ANDROGYNY AND SELF-SUFFICIENT NARCISSISM

auch nicht den Mann, sondern etwas Wunderbares dazwischen. Und das Wunderbare war ich." (374)* Here, Krull explicitly acknowledges that he is this extraordinary intermediate being. The implication of this characterization is that what is neither male nor female is either divine or androgynous or, most probably, both. We discern here echoes of a motif sounded at the beginning of "Der junge Joseph" where Mann speaks of youthful beauty, as in the case of Joseph, forever hovering between the masculine and the feminine: "Ein Jüngling von siebzehn ist nicht schön im Sinne vollkommener Männlichkeit. Er ist auch nicht schön im Sinne einer bloß unpraktischen Weiblichkeit – die wenigsten würde das anziehen. Aber soviel ist zuzugeben, daß Schönheit als Jugendanmut seelisch und ausdrucksweise immer ein wenig ins Weibliche spielt..." (IV, 394)** This idea underscores the basically androgynous character of youthful beauty with its slight predominance of the feminine aspect. It explains, to be sure, Stürzli's curious confusion of sexual instinct; but more importantly, it suggests a parallel to the primal Hermes in whose original

---

* "Enthusiasts who are in search of neither a woman nor a man, but some extraordinary being in between. And I was this extraordinary being."

** "A male youth of seventeen is not beautiful in the sense of perfect masculinity. He is also not beautiful in the sense of sheer impractical femininity – few would find that attractive. It must be conceded, however, that beauty in the guise of youthful grace always inclines both inwardly and outwardly toward the feminine."

bisexuality the feminine aspect is predominant.

Krull's androgyny has numerous archetypal precedents. Divine bisexuality, particularly in the cosmogonic gods, is a consistent motif in primitive mythologies and in comparative religion. Mircea Eliade notes that the divinities of cosmic fertility are either hermaphroditic or alternate between male and female sex in successive agricultural years.[2] Bisexuality is common to such vegetation divinities as Attis, Adonis, and Dionysos, and is also characteristic of the Earth Mother (Cybele). The primal god is androgynous in the primitive religions of China, India, Egypt, and Australia as well as in Germanic mythology (Odin, Loki, Tuisco). The Gnostic doctrine of the hermaphroditic Primordial Man found its way into early Christianity and provided the source for the idea that Adam was originally bisexual, since he carried Eve hidden within him.[3] Jung interprets in Christian allegory the motif of the woman sprung from Christ's right side as suggesting that Jesus is here interpreted as the second Adam.[4] Christ's androgyny is evident in much of religious art where his image is generally not unambiguously masculine, and medieval iconography sometimes goes so far as to depict Christ with female breasts.[5] The ubiquity and historical continuity of the motif of androgyny attests to its archetypal status. But divine androgyny is part of a larger, more fundamental mythological concept – the paradoxical coexistence of contraries in the divinity. Ancient man's experience of the divinity is ambivalent. By turns or even simultaneously the divinity is both good and evil, benevolent and terrible, creative and destructive. Similarly, in religious experience the Judaeo-Christian Yaweh is both kind and wrathful, and in Christian mysticism and theology this divine ambivalence led to Nicholas of Cusa's formulation of the term *coincidentia oppositorum* as a designation for the simultaneous existence and transcendence of antitheses in God.[6] The union of all conceivable opposites in God constitutes a mystery, while at the same time it signifies the totality and perfection of the divinity. Viewed in these terms, divine androgyny is the union of the most striking opposites and perhaps the most perfect symbol of wholeness and self-sufficiency.

Analogous to the mythical model, Krull's androgyny is but one form of a basic duality and indeterminateness of his character which gives rise to ambivalent responses in persons of his social environment. The oddities connected with his various talents and the dubious social standing of his parents make him the object of dark and contemptuous glances among the small-town bourgeoisie. But in these glances there is also mingled an expression of reluctant admiration. His parodistic glibness is occasion for the hotel clerk to remark that he seems either a fool or possibly a little too intelligent. It is basically characteristic of Krull up to the time of his assumption of Marquis de Venosta's identity that he remains indeterminate or ambiguous as to character and status in the eyes of society. Essentially an artistic and protean personality, he defies all classification into a conventional bourgeois scheme. Ambivalence is the natural response to indeterminateness. Whatever resists classification or does not conform to typology or categorization is the source of either vexation or fascination or both. It seems that the collective psychological security of the bourgeoisie is dependent upon the presentation of an unequivocal face.

The ambiguity of his identity in virtually every situation in which he finds himself and in every role he plays is the source of keen, ironic delight for Krull. The real Marquis de Venosta best sums this up when he says: "Während Ihr Pikendienst Sie als einen Angehörigen der unteren Klassen erscheinen läßt – es muß Ihnen geradezu Spaß machen, denke ich mir –, halten Sie natürlich innerlich an Ihrem Stande als Gentleman fest und kehren zwischendurch auch äußerlich zu ihm zurück, wie heute abend." (502)*

The ambivalent responses provoked by the ambiguity of Krull's outward appearance and behavior are matched by the inner contradictions of his personality. Krull's attitude toward the world is reciprocally ambivalent. On more than

---

* "While your service in the ranks makes you appear to be a member of the lower classes – I can imagine that you must find this positively amusing – you of course hold inwardly to your status of gentleman and return to it outwardly from time to time, as you are doing this evening."

one occasion he admits that his basic attitude toward society is contradictory. This ambitendency generally manifests itself in his eagerness to be on affectionate terms with society on the one hand, and a coolness, critical reserve, and even social withdrawal, on the other. These opposing tendencies may succeed each other by turns as the result of a pendulum swing, but more often than not they appear to be held simultaneously in delicate equilibrium. The period in which he becomes the object of dark and contemptuous glances from his fellow townsmen reinforces his tendency toward misanthropy and withdrawal from the world which, as he says, "... von jeher meinem Charakterbilde angehaftet hatte und mit werbender Anhänglichkeit an Welt und Menschen so einträchtig Hand in Hand zu gehen vermag." (328)* At the Stoudebecker Circus in Paris he characterizes his impression of the artistic feats in such a way as to leave no doubt about his markedly ambivalent attitude: "Wohl entging mir nichts, wohl nahm ich inständig prüfend jede Einzelheit in mich. Es war Hingebung, aber sie hatte... etwas Aufsässiges... meine Seele... übte einen Gegendruck aus gegen die sie bestürmenden Eindrücke, es war ... bei aller Bewunderung etwas von Bosheit in ihrem eindringlichen Be-

---

* "... had always been a part of my character pattern and which is able to coexist so harmoniously with solicitous attachment to the world and its people."

trachten der Tricks, Künste, Wirkungen." (463)*

Those of Krull's societal relationships which are based on mutual affection are in themselves contradictory, since they are generally bipolar in terms of social class. His inherent aristocratic propensity and elitist-consciousness which draw him into mutually sympathetic relations with persons of noble status – Lord Kilmarnock and Marquis de Venosta – contrast radically with his friendly associations with prostitutes (Rozsa) and underworld characters (Stanko). Of Hermes it is said that "he runs around the earth and enjoys equally the company of the good and the wicked."[7] It is noteworthy, however, that Mann diverges somewhat from the mythic prototype in depicting Krull not as the patron of thieves but of prostitutes. This is clearly evident when Krull refuses complicity in Stanko's proposed burglary of a villa in a wealthy suburb of Paris. All Krull's societal relationships are characterized by this natural gravitation toward polar opposites, toward the top and bottom rungs of the social ladder, while all mediocracy is consciously eschewed. In one instance it is an extremely sly and ironic joke that Krull ascends the ladder in order to establish

---

* "Nothing, to be sure, escaped my attention. I took in every detail passionately and scrutinizingly. It was surrender, but there was something rebellious about it... my soul exerted a counterpressure against the overwhelming assault of impressions. For all my admiration, there was a certain spitefulness in this penetrating scrutiny of the tricks and arts and their effects."

contact with an "underworld" character – Master Pierre Jean-Pierre. The watchmaker's pawnshop is located in the Rue de l'Échelle au Ciel (literally, Ladder to Heaven Avenue). Prostitution as a social institution is compatible within the orbit of Krull's associations because of the ambiguity of both its legal and moral status. It is here that the patronage of both underworld and well-heeled society converge. Complicity in burglary with Stanko, by contrast, would incur the stigma of unequivocal moral reprehensibility and thus constitute a violent disruption of Krull's delicately ambiguous style of life and moral code. In principle, only that which is ambiguous and ambivalent fits into the total pattern of Krull's actions. The unequivocal is consistently avoided as something alien and incompatible.

Krull's ambitendency – critical withdrawal versus sociability – is the expression of an underlying conflict between introversion and extraversion. This conflict derives from the very nucleus of his character – narcissism. Indeed, there is hardly a behavior pattern or aspect of Krull's development that does not relate significantly to this center of his personality. Narcissism, in Freudian terms, is essentially the direction of libidinal energy on to the ego instead of an outside love-object.[8] It stems from an idealization of the ego and involves the inability to love anything that does not pertain to the self. Jung compares the libido to a "steady stream pouring its waters into the world of reality."[9] In Krull's narcissism this flow of libido is regulated by the dynamics of an inner resistance. Ego-consciousness is in perpetual conflict with the objective reality of society, resulting in an antagonism and unresolved dialectic tension between psychic forces. On the one hand, there appears to be a centrifugal force of the psyche desiring social intercourse, while another opposing centripetal force, owing to the basic opposition between ego and society, causes the libido to flow back to the subjective world of fantasy where ego gratification is keener.

The dialectic of this whole process crops up early in the work. Krull connects his reluctance to exchange the darkness of the womb at birth for the light of day with his extraordinary gift and passion for sleep. The womb and sleep are both symbols of the unconscious. But more significantly, Freud connects sleep with narcissism.[10] Sleep implies a narcissistic withdrawal of libidinal interest from objects of the external world (reality) on to the subject's own self (ego). Krull is therefore perfectly right when he remarks that there might seem to be a contradiction between this love of sleep and his great impulse toward life and love. The contradiction is precisely that between narcissism (introversion) and social or amorous involvement (extraversion). But after devoting much thought to this matter, Krull says, he has come to the conclusion that this involves not a contradiction, but rather a hidden connection and correspondence. Krull does not go on to explain how this is possible, but what he probably has in mind is the idea that self-love or self-regard is the prerequisite for love of others. Krull attempts later in the work to equate love for others as self-love directed outward. According to Freudian psychology, such a situation is possible, but its virtuous quality is highly dubious, for it implies nothing more than a transference of narcissism to the external object or person. In this case a person loves in conformity with his own narcissism or ego-ideal, in that he may love what he once *was* and no longer *is* or he may love what possesses the qualities he never had at all.

Narcissistic self-regard, according to Freud, is not only sustained but also enhanced by every achievement that confirms the narcissist's feeling of omnipotence or self-sufficiency. This dynamic is constantly operative in Krull's development. His experiments with the supernatural aspects of the human will and his efforts at simulation and deception are consistently crowned with success, which reinforces his ego aggrandizement and his conviction that he is endowed with extraordinary powers. Concomitant with this reinforcement of Krull's narcissism is an intensification of the alienation of the ego from society. Just as the repeated experience of success corroborates ego-idealization and self-regard, so also does being loved by others enhance narcissism. Krull's narcissism is nurtured by the fact that he consistently seeks to please and to be loved to the exclusion of giving love. "The aim and the satisfaction in a narcissistic object-choice," Freud says, "is to be loved."[11]

DIVINE ANDROGYNY AND SELF-SUFFICIENT NARCISSISM

If we now consider the converse of these preconditions for narcissism, it becomes apparent that experiences of failure and of not being loved lower self-regard and are ultimately inimical to the subsistence of narcissism. It is conspicuous that Krull never experiences anything that he regards as a substantial failure. His lack of success at school does not trouble him, for at bottom he has sincere contempt for the regimentalized style of this institution and finds it incompatible with his positive insistence on freedom of behavior and imagination. On the other hand, there are circumstances that threaten to deflate his ego, in which case the libido is activated toward the object. This happens, for example, when the invitation he extends to one of his classmates to visit him at his house meets with a rebuff because of the ill-repute of Krull's family. About this Krull says: "Das schmerzte mich und ließ mir einen Umgang begehrenswert erscheinen, an dem mir sonst nichts gelegen gewesen wäre." (276)*

The dynamics of narcissism involve a deflection from sexuality. Just as Krull presents an androgynous image to the world as a result of a physiognomic duality, so also can his own sexuality be called ambiguous. The sexual aspect of Krull's behavior is presented in a most equivocal and deceptive guise. For while it is true that he repeatedly assures the reader that he is erotically

---

* "This hurt me and made me crave a type of company that otherwise would not have meant anything to me."

DIVINE ANDROGYNY AND SELF-SUFFICIENT NARCISSISM

gifted, and prides himself on deriving pleasures from sexual relations that far transcend the ordinary, there is no evidence that his sexuality is anything more than passive. The turning point is his assumption of Venosta's identity, but prior to this there is no instance of Krull's active pursuit of amorous relations. This is true of both the affair with Genovefa, the family maid, and with Rozsa, the Hungarian prostitute. In the former case the incident is described with the utmost of vagueness and circumlocution as to the instigating circumstances. For Krull, indulgence seems more a matter of exploration and ego-fulfillment than of sexual drive or passion. Krull's description of ecstasy – while it is probably parodistic and therefore not to be taken too literally – is still somewhat embarrassing: "... so entzieht sich das markverzehrende, wahrhaft unerhörte Vergnügen, das ich an Genovefa's weißer und wohlgenährter Brust erprobte, jedenfalls aller Beschreibung. Ich schrie und glaubte gen Himmel zu fahren." (314)* The "well-nourished breast" is a mother symbol and suggests regression to infantile narcissism, a withdrawal from the conscious to the unconscious, a return to shelter and security. The passage carries a strong import of sexual immaturity; eroticism is the product of narcissistic transference. Krull succeeds here in possessing the

* "The all-consuming and truly unprecedented pleasures I savored on Genovefa's white and well-nourished breast defy all description. I cried out and felt myself rising toward heaven."

heterosexual object which, within the context of narcissism, means an enhancement of ego and self-regard. Yet, the epilogue to this erotic interlude makes it quite clear that deflection from sexuality is more consistent with Krull's personality: "Ich für meinen Teil kenne viele feinere, köstlichere, verflüchtigtere Arten der Genugtuung als die derbe Handlung, die zuletzt doch nur eine beschränkte und trügerische Abspeisung des Verlangens bedeutet, und ich meine, daß derjenige sich wenig auf das Glück versteht, dessen Trachten nur geradeswegs auf dies Ziel gerichtet ist. Das meine ging stets ins Große, Ganze und Weite, es fand feine, würzige Sättigung, wo andere sie nicht suchen würden, es war von jeher wenig spezialisiert oder genau bestimmt, und dies ist eine der Ursachen, weshalb ich trotz inbrünstiger Veranlagung so lange unwissend und unschuldig, ja eigentlich zeit meines Lebens ein Kind und Träumer verblieb." (315)*

* "I, for my part, know many kinds of satisfaction that are finer, more exquisite and more subtle than this crude act which, in the final analysis, is nothing more than a limited and illusory gratification of desire; I believe that a person whose energies are directed point-blank to this goal alone does not know what delight really is. My appetites always encompassed a larger radius, they found delicate and piquant satisfaction where others would not think of looking; they were never precisely defined or specialized, and this is one of the reasons why I, despite a most ardent disposition, remained for such a long time ignorant and innocent. In fact, all my life I have remained a child and a dreamer."

In the experience with Rozsa the accent is on Krull's possession of superior gifts in the art of loving, which induces one to overlook the actual fact that he is receiving practical sex education. Krull's erotic role is here again decidedly passive: "Die Vertraute hatte eine Art, ihr Bein über meines zu legen, als kreuze sie nur ihre eigenen; alles, was sie sagte und tat, war wundersam ungehemmt, kühn und fessellos... und mit freudiger Leichtigkeit tat ich's ihr gleich." (380)* Krull is the seduced rather than the seducer. Perhaps the best commentary on Krull's erotic passivity is the evasive answer he gives to Venosta's point-blank question: "Haben Sie jemals leidenschaftlich geliebt?" And Krull: "Ich bin ganz gut in der Lage, Ihnen zu folgen, Marquis." Venosta continues: "Daß Sie in Liebesdingen Bescheid wissen, glaube ich ohne Ihre Versicherung. Und doch scheinen Sie mir der Typ, der mehr geliebt wird, als daß er selber liebte. Habe ich unrecht? Gut, lassen wir's in der Schwebe." (505)**

* "My intimate companion had a way of putting her leg over mine as though she were merely crossing her own; everything she said and did was marvellously uninhibited, bold, and free... and with joyous facility I matched her advances."
** "Have you ever been passionately in love?" "I'm in a very good position to follow you, Marquis." "Even without your assurance, I believe that you know all about matters of love. And yet you seem to me the type who is more loved than loving. Am I wrong? All right, let's leave that question undecided."

The ambiguity of Krull's sexuality is suggested by the absence of any definite orientation toward heterosexual erotism on the one hand and his unmistakable rejection of homosexual advances on the other. This implies an intermediate or neutral position of asexuality, which is to be understood in the sense of a disinterested or non-libidinal attitude toward erotic love. Krull's narcissistic energies are directed toward being loved. Krull does not actually love, for loving, in the sense of a transference of libidinal energy on to another object, would be in his case tantamount to a lowering of ego-idealization. In Krull's narcissism object-libido is repressed in favor of ego-libido. "When libido is repressed," Freud says, "the erotic cathexis is felt as a severe depletion of the ego, the satisfaction of love is impossible, and the re-enrichment of the ego can be effected only by a withdrawal of libido from its objects."[12] Narcissism thus constitutes the permanent domicile to which the stray libido constantly returns. This unresolved dialectic persists as long as narcissism prevails. A synthesis of object-libido and ego-libido is not reached until after Krull assumes his new identity of marquis. This decisive reorientation and the forces that contribute to it will be discussed in subsequent chapters. We must first turn to an assessment of an experience that constitutes an important antecedent to this change of identity and its concomitant change in orientation. This vitally important happening is the encounter with Madame Houpflé.

V. DIANA THE PROVIDER

However ludicrous and burlesque the Madame Houpflé episode may appear on the surface, it is of central importance to Krull's development. It marks, first of all, the beginning of a conscious identification with Hermes in contrast to an unconscious imitation of the archetypal personality prior to this experience. Secondly, Diane Philibert bestows upon Krull the material means which make it possible for him to assume outwardly a new form of material existence which eventually leads to the assumption of a new identity – that of Marquis de Venosta. Diane Philibert thus constitutes a crucially important link between Krull's old and new personality. Externally, this change of *persona* involves the discarding of beggar's rags for riches. Of more profound significance is the fact that her intervention initiates the transition from Krull's egocentric isolation and narcissism to an awareness of universal sympathy and altruistic love. In assuming Marquis de Venosta's identity Krull not only changes his name and social status but a certain vital part of his psychological constitution as well. The experience with Diane Philibert is comparable enough, on the mythological plane, to the arousal of full masculine sexuality in the primal Hermes to suggest a situation of parallel importance. In both cases we are dealing with the emergence of a latent and passive characteristic which ascends to a status of unequivocal dominance and thereby resolves erotic ambiguity. The psychosexual machinery is set in motion for the eventual conversion from the private, self-centered concerns of narcissism to a universally-oriented consciousness.

The figure of Diane Philibert is a refracted and condensed image of a mythic prototype: Artemis. This is obliquely suggested by the fact that her mythological namesake is the corresponding Roman divinity, Diana. Like the Greek Artemis, with whom she was always identified, Diana is known chiefly in her capacity as the goddess of the wilderness and woodlands, and as the chief huntress to the gods. She is associated with nature in general, but particularly with the teeming life of nature and thus ultimately with fertility and childbirth. She is a great benefactress to farmers, filling their barns with a rich supply of fruits and multiplying their cattle. Related to this particular quality is her maternal solicitude. She is the preserver and protectress, both of young wild game and youth, especially young boys. Walter F. Otto points out that at Elis there was a sanctuary of Artemis near the gymnasium where she was called "friend of boys," and that young ephebi held festal processions in her honor, especially in Athens.[1] Artemis is a guardian of growing youth and has a special interest in youth entering upon maturity.

These are all positive traits. But the image of Artemis-Diana would be grossly incomplete without mentioning the negative, dark side of her nature which always stands in counterbalance and thus corresponds to the typical duality and ambivalence of divinities. Because of her identification – in the later poets – with Hecate, the Goddess of the Dark and of the Moon, Artemis becomes associated with sinister deeds of darkness, thus vividly incorporating the ambiguity of good and evil. This identification most probably derived from the fact that Artemis was Apollo's twin sister. Many of her epithets reveal that she was considered the feminine counterpart to Apollo. Artemis was the goddess of the Moon, Apollo the god of the Sun. Apollo symbolized spiritual freedom and distance and bore the significant appellation of *hekatos*, "the hitter from afar", an epithet to which Thomas Mann refers in his essay on the art of the novel as a symbol of objectivity and irony.[2] Significantly, Artemis also bears the epithet in its feminine form, *hekate*. Her shafts hit their mark from afar, whether the target be wild game or human warriors. Artemis as Hecate is the wild huntress stalking at night. Hecate plays a significant role in the syncretism of Greek myth. She becomes identified not only with Brimo, the underworldly mother, but also with Persephone – the daughter of Demeter – who, after being abducted by Pluto, became the queen of Hades. These identifications are of great significance for my interpretation, for they not only serve to explain and reconcile apparent discrepancies between the natures of Artemis and Diane Philibert, but they also provide a basis for what would otherwise seem to be an impossible identification of Madame Houpflé with Zouzou who, as we shall see later, corresponds to Persephone in the Demeter myth. We are dealing here with a web of complex identifications and syncretistic regroupings typical of the interchangeability of personages in the fluid world of myth and, significantly, of Mann's novel as well. Hecate, then, represents the dark, terrible, and sinister side of Diana. While Diana may on the one hand appear as the chaste virgin, Hecate may degrade herself to the level of a whore. We will recall that in the mythologem of the primal Hermes as bisexual, Artemis is mentioned as one of the three arousers of his male sexuality. Accordingly, it seems more plausible to ascribe this deed to the Hecate-side of Artemis rather than to her quality of unapproachable virgin.

In the *Golden Bough*, Frazer relates a story about Diana which suggests that she may have become a huntress of a special sort – the searcher for a male consort. Owing to the curious circumstance that Diana was a goddess of fertility and yet a virgin, it was thought that she should have a male partner, apparently on the assumption that she who causes fertility should also be fertilized. "The aim of their union," Frazer says, "would be to promote the fruitfulness of the earth, of animals, and of mankind; and it might naturally be thought that this object would be more surely attained if the sacred nuptials were celebrated every year, the parts of the divine bride and bridegroom being played either by their images or by living persons."[3]

Though by no means a virgin, Madame Houpflé prefers, as an authoress and representative of the

DIANA THE PROVIDER

intellect, to write under her *maiden* name, Diane Philibert. This establishes her duality of character – as Diane she is the virgin, and as Madame Houpflé she is Hecate, the aggressive and lascivious nymph. We first encounter her as a traveler (traveling can be a symbol of erotic longing), and later it becomes apparent that she is an itinerant "huntress" in search of a beautiful youthful lover. It is Krull who first (unwittingly) alludes to the quest motif: "Ihre Nähe im engen Raum des Fahrstuhls benahm mir recht eigentümlich den Sinn. Ohne von mir zu wissen, ohne mich je gesehen zu haben, ohne meiner auch jetzt gewahr zu werden, trug sie mich gestaltlos in ihren Gedanken seit dem Augenblick, gestern abend oder heute morgen, wo ihr beim Ausleeren ihres Koffers das Fehlen des Kästchens auffällig geworden war." (419)* The situation in which the seeker is unwittingly so close to the object of her search enchants Krull to the highest degree. After he has become brightened in appearance by his purchase of a new outfit of clothing, Krull is content when thinking of "die Frau, die mich bildlos im Sinne trug und nun ... einem Bilde

---

* "Her standing close to me in the narrow space of the elevator had a peculiar effect on my senses. Without knowing about me, without ever having seen me, without being aware of me now, she had been carrying me featureless in her thoughts from the moment – last night or this morning – when she discovered, while unpacking her suitcase, that her little jewel case was missing."

nachfragte, das ihrer und ihres Fragens würdiger war als bisher." (430)*

Krull's repeated reference to the "gestaltloses Bild" ("featureless image") bears an affinity with the Jungian characterization of the archetype. In its original state, the archetype is essentially a form or image lacking in solid or well-defined content. It acquires solidity and eventual consciousness in the actual encounter with the empirical object.[4] Diane thus carries within her the primordial image of the youthful beauty of the ephebus. By her own confession she is drawn erotically only to young boys – a sexual refraction of the maternal tenderness and loving care which Artemis bestowed upon young boys approaching maturity. "Willst du glauben, Geliebter," she says to Krull, "daß ich nur dich, immer nur dich geliebt habe, seit ich empfinde? Will sagen, natürlich nicht dich, doch die Idee von dir, den holden Augenblick, den du verkörperst?... Nur euch Knaben hab' ich geliebt von je..." (445)** The maternal motive may also figure here. Diane speculates that perhaps this devious passion is "versetzte Mutterliebe, die Sehnsucht nach dem

---

* "The woman who bore my featureless image in her mind and was now searching for a figure more worthy of her quest than heretofore."

** "Would you believe, beloved, that I have loved only you, never anyone but you, since I have been able to feel? By that I mean, of course, not you, but the idea of you, the lovely moment which you embody... From the beginning I have loved only you boys."

Sohn" ("transferred mother-love, the yearning for a son"), for she had never been a mother, had never borne a son. Artemis as huntress, her maternal solicitude, and her favor toward young boys are mythic motifs which merge here, translated into the psychoanalytical.

Nowhere in the *Confessions* is Mann so boldly specific in his description of erotic stimulation as in the Diane episode. It is evident that he abandons here the prissy reserve and cautious, fastidious approach to sex characteristic of the Genovefa episode. All of this is conspicuously absent in Krull's remark: "... daß meine Männlichkeit, wie ihr nicht entgehen konnte, in den bedrängendsten Aufstand geriet." (441)* This is a re-enactment of the archetypal situation – the arousal of Hermes' sexuality – which is described by Cicero in his *De natura deorum* as follows: "Mercurius unus Caelo patre, Die matre natus, cuius obscenius excitata natura traditur, quod aspectu Proserpinae commotus sit." (III 22,56) To avoid confusion, we should translate the names into Greek: Mercury is Hermes, Proserpina is Persephone who is often confused with Artemis.[5] It is this phallic excitation in Hermes to which Kerenyi attributes symbolic significance. It signifies, in his interpretation, the emergence of Hermes' fully matured, emancipated, and unambiguous male sexuality. But it also implies,

---

* "... that my manhood, as she could not fail to notice, passed into a state of most urgent arousal."

I believe, the *separation* of Hermes from his hermaphroditic relationship to Aprodite in which the feminine principle had hitherto been predominant. In the absence of any specific documentary evidence, it is impossible to settle the question whether the inseparable connection between Hermes and Aphrodite is to be understood in the sense of unicorporal fusion or whether Hermes is to be conceived of as bisexual or androgynous, that is, as the embodiment of the male and the female principles in himself alone. The two possibilities are not mutually exclusive. But to insist on a neat distinction would be tantamount to a confusion of scientific positivism with the syncretism and polyvalent symbolism of myth. In Hermes the arousal of masculinity symbolizes the primal origin of the male sex as distinct from the female. The differentiation of the sexes, in myth and in religion, proceeds by separation. In Genesis, God creates Eve by *separating* her from Adam. Etymologically, the word *sex* is a derivative of the Latin verb *secare* 'to cut', hence 'to separate.' The process of separation is synonymous with the act of creation and with a dawning consciousness – the consciousness of individual identity.

As the arouser of Krull's masculinity and "manhood," the role of Diane Philibert corresponds to that of the mythical Artemis-Hecate – she is a recurrence of the primordial feminine source of the absolute male principle. The term "male principle" refers here to the emergence of a dormant and passive characteristic which had

DIANA THE PROVIDER

hitherto been subordinate to the feminine principle. Krull's sexuality, like his identity as a whole, had been indeterminate. Diane calls him "Mignon in Livree." (441) "Mignon" is not merely denotative in meaning. It is very likely an allusion to the young female character in Goethe's *Wilhelm Meister*, an androgynous being, whose sex remains for a long time not definitely established. That Diane elicits the masculine in Krull is also implicit in her calling him "kühner Knecht" ("daring menial"). (438) This prompts Krull to reflect: "Das packende Wort ["kühner Knecht"] lag mir den ganzen Abend im Sinn... Es kränkte mich etwas, das Wort, und erfüllte mich doch auch wieder mit Stolz – sogar auf meine Kühnheit, die ich gar nicht besessen, sondern die sie mir einfach unterstellt und zudiktiert hatte. Jedenfalls besaß ich sie nun im Überfluß. Sie hatte sie mir eingeflößt...." (439)* In Krull, phallic excitation is a symbol of the emergence of the dominance of the male principle, of the resolution of ambiguous sexuality and ambiguous identity. Not only that: it coincides also with Krull's first awareness of his mythical identity with Hermes which Diane also imputes to him. With the sun-

---

* "This thrilling phrase ['daring menial'] lay in my mind all evening. It offended me a little, this phrase, and yet at the same time it made me proud – even of the daring which I had not possessed at all, but which she had simply imputed to me and placed under my commmand. At any rate, I now possessed it in superabundance. She had inspired it in me."

dering of androgyny comes the consciousness of a specific individual identity. Krull's earlier divinations of his godlike status are transformed into reality. But here the typical and the individual merge into one, for Krull realizes that his existence has a mythological precedent – Hermes – of whom he is the reincarnation.

The emergence of Krull's psychosexual maturity prepares the way for, but does not yet involve, an alteration in the relation between ego-libido and object-libido to the extent that narcissism or autoerotism is abandoned for genuine love. Such a change is as yet ruled out by Diane's own conception of love as a perversion. That she herself shows signs of being sexually perverse conforms to the Hecate-side of her nature. She is unmistakably masochistic in her desire to be physically beaten and to be degraded by being called a whore (coprolalia). Of the mythical Hecate it is said that she indulged in the crudest and basest forms of eroticism.[6]

The merging of ego-libido and object-libido in Krull does not take place until his encounter with Zouzou (Persephone), though it is Diane who prepares the way for this experience. Consistent with her Artemis-nature as the multiplier of cattle and grain, she bestows upon Krull the necessary material means which will enable him to assume the identity of Marquis de Venosta in which outward social status complements inner substance. Diane Philibert is the provider, indeed, the multiplier, of Krull's riches. Her bizarre command that he exercise his rights as the god of thieves by stealing all of her jewelry and cash provides him with a "Liebes-Diebsgut" ("treasure trove of love and theft") for which he receives from Master Pierre Jean-Pierre six thousand francs and innumerable pats on the shoulder. This gesture of approval on the part of the watchmaker hints at another Hermes-capacity which Krull here fulfills: the patron of commerce. For Krull, the treasure trove is a veritable windfall, a sudden and wholly unexpected stroke of luck. In Greek the word for any kind of windfall is *hermaion*.[7] The etymological relationship of this word to *Hermes* is significant, for it reflects *in nuce* one of his outstanding attributes – the god of unexpected gain. Any sudden stroke of good luck, such as finding valuables on the road, was interpreted as coming from Hermes, to whom thanks were due. This would not seem to preclude the possibility that Hermes himself could be favored by such luck.

Bulfinch relates two myths about Diana and the fair youth Endymion which contain in condensed form a number of points of oblique resemblance to Krull's Diana-experience.[8] Endymion was a beautiful shepherd youth who tended his flock on Mount Latmos. One night Diana, the Moon, looked down and saw him sleeping. As the virgin goddess of the moon, her heart was cold, but the sight of his surpassing beauty warmed her so much that she came down to him, kissed him, and watched over him (motif of maternal solicitude) while he slept. The other story tells how Jupiter endowed Endymion with the gift of perpetual youth united with perpetual sleep. Diana took care that his fortunes should not suffer by his inactive life. She caused his flock to increase and guarded it from wild beasts.

VI. THE ELEUSINIAN MYSTERIES REVISITED

With the assumption of his final new identity, that of Marquis de Venosta, Krull embarks on what was to have been an odyssey of classical dimensions. That it turned out to be so geographically abridged, terminating as it does at its first station – Lisbon, can hardly be the fault of Thomas Mann. For a story such as Krull's – particularly in view of the universal dimension it had already assumed and was still implying – is interminable. I find it very significant, however, that the novel ends where it does – in Krull's embrace with Senhora Kuckuck – for, as I intend to show, this ending is decidedly not arbitrary. It is indeed a fitting and logical conclusion in terms of the mythic motif which Mann was utilizing – the return to the Archetypal Feminine, to the Great Mother. The dreams of primordial unity evoked by the enchanting spectacle of the brother-sister pair on the balcony of the Frankfurt hotel are symbolically fulfilled in this embrace with the Archetypal Mother. It is the object of the hero's quest, and beyond this act of consummation the story, on the mythic plane, cannot meaningfully progress.

Krull's fascination with the double-image of mother and daughter is prefigured in the earlier experience of the double-image of brother and sister. They are slightly foreign in appearance, dark-haired, and, as Krull speculates, they might be Spanish, Portuguese, South American, Argentinian, or Brazilian. That the pair consists of brother and sister rather than mother and daughter is a variation on the theme of complementaries, of unity in duality. The image excites in Krull dreams of love, a longing for union, for primal indivisibility and indeterminateness which – translated into the language of myth – is the primordial androgynous or bisexual character of Man. But since Krull himself embodies the androgynous principle, his longing may strike us as paradoxical. Is he not longing for something he already possesses? Not quite. Aside from any question about the degree to which he is conscious of the primordial unity which his androgynous cast symbolizes, his unity is valid only on the level of self-sufficient narcissism. It is incomplete, this unity, to the extent that it lacks a vital ingredient – love and universal sympathy. Hence the accent in this dream symbolism is on the longing for union brought about by love. But Krull's vision and ideal of love at this point is still narcissistic and anti-social: "Nur an den beiden Polen menschlicher Verbindung," he says in the epilogue to the spectacle of the brother-sister pair, "dort, wo es noch keine oder keine Worte mehr gibt, im Blick und in der Umarmung, ist eigentlich das Glück zu finden, denn nur dort ist Unbedingtheit, Freiheit, Geheimnis und tiefe Rücksichtslosigkeit. Alles, was an Verkehr und Austausch dazwischenliegt, ist flau und lau, ist durch Förmlichkeit und bürgerliche Übereinkunft bestimmt, bedingt und beschränkt. Hier herrscht das Wort..." (348)*

* "Only at the two opposite poles of human contact, where there are no words or no more words, in the glance

Ego-consciousness is still in conflict with society, and the *sine qua non* of existence is freedom without responsibility. Krull's interest lies in "den äußersten, schweigsamen Regionen menschlicher Beziehung... wo Fremdheit und bürgerliche Bezuglosigkeit noch einen freien Urzustand aufrechterhalten und die Blicke unverantwortlich, in traumhafter Unkeuschheit sich vermählen; dann aber der anderen, wo die möglichste Vereinigung, Vertraulichkeit und Vermischung jenen wortlosen Urzustand auf das vollkommenste wiederherstellt." (349)*

As a desideratum of the love-experience, such a condition is woefully inadequate. It is love on the Hecate-level, and finds its almost literal fulfillment in the encounter with Rozsa, the prostitute. Love without involvement, without the banal preliminaries that involve speech and courtship – such an "ideal" is capable of realization only in sexual relations with a whore. Krull and in the embrace, is happiness really to be found, for only in these do we find the absolute, do we find freedom, mystery, and profound ruthlessness. Everything by way of intercourse and exchange that lies in between is lukewarm and insipid; it is determined, conditioned, and limited by formality and middle-class convention. Here words rule over everything."

* "... the extreme, silent regions of human relations... where unfamiliarity and social rootlessness still maintain a free, primordial condition and glances meet and marry irresponsibly in dreamlike unchastity; but then, too, the other in which the greatest possible union, intimacy, and commingling restore most completely that wordless primordial condition."

meets Rozsa in a medium-grade café. They exchange glances, she favors him with a signal, "jenen seitlichen Wink ins Buhlerisch-Ungewisse," (379)* and they leave. From the very beginning, Krull says, this affair had the "unbedingte, enthobene und entbundene Unverantwortlichkeit, die sonst nur dem Traum eigentümlich ist, wo unser Ich mit Schatten ohne gültiges Eigenleben, mit Erzeugnissen seiner selbst verkehrt..." (380)** The implication of narcissistic transference is evident. Krull's ego-ideal is projected on to this experience. In Rozsa he perceives characteristics which are akin to his own – her eyes shimmer with an *indeterminate* color, the direction of their gaze is also *indeterminate*. On the other hand, she possesses complementary traits that he lacks – an uncomplicated and uninhibited instinct for sociability: "alles, was sie sagte und tat, war wundersam ungehemmt, kühn und fessellos... und mit freudiger Leichtigkeit tat ich's ihr gleich." (380)*** What Krull learns from Rozsa's school of practical sex education is "nicht sowohl... eine Verfeinerung *in* der Liebe, als... eine solche *durch*

---

* "... that sidewise nod toward the licentious and the unknown..."
** "... unconditional, free, and uncommitted irresponsibility that is usually characteristic only of dreams, where our ego associates with shadows that have no independent existence, with creations of its own."
*** "Everything she said and did was marvellously uninhibited, bold, and free... and with joyous facility I matched her advances."

die Liebe..." (384)* The italics are Krull's, and, as he points out, they emphasize an important distinction. The first amounts to a refinement in technique, whereas the second suggests the completion of a phase in the development toward psychosexual maturity. The seeds which Rozsa implants in him are brought to fruition by Diane Philibert.

Related to the experience of the brother-sister pair is the appearance of another remarkable figure – Andromache. In her the idea of androgynous unity is incorporated in a single person. As the first half of her name suggests, the masculine element is predominant in her, which makes her the complementary counterpart, in feminine form, to Krull's androgyny which, prior to the Diane-experience, inclines toward a predominance of the feminine principle. In the figure of Andromache we meet with the closest approximation to the sculptured hermaphrodite figure in Greek art. This is at once evident in Krull's description of her: "Sie war von etwas mehr als mittlerer Weibesgröße... Ihre Brust war geringfügig, ihr Becken schmal, die Muskulatur ihrer Arme, wie sich versteht, stärker ausgebildet als sonst bei Frauen, und ihre greifenden Hände zwar nicht von männlicher Größe, aber doch auch nicht klein genug, um die Frage ganz auszuschalten, ob sie, in Gottes Namen, denn vielleicht heimlich ein Jüngling sei. Nein, die weibliche Artung ihrer Brust war

* .... not only a refinement *in* love but also *through* love..."

immerhin unzweideutig, und so doch auch, bei aller Schlankheit, die Form ihrer Schenkel. Sie lächelte kaum. Ihre schönen Lippen, fern von Verpreßtheit, standen meist leicht geöffnet, aber das taten freilich auch, gespannt, die Flügel ihrer griechisch gestalteten, ein wenig niedergehenden Nase." (459)* Understandably enough, the only element lacking in this otherwise virtually complete description of the classical hermaphrodite is the presence of the male genitals. It is not necessary to press the matter of anatomical similarity this far. In the first place, the sculptured hermaphrodite is generally either unclad or thinly draped, whereas Andromache's performance requires her to conform to civilized standards of wearing clothing. As a living embodiment of a radically complete hermaphrodite, the figure of Andromache would constitute a stark anatomical aberration, a monstrosity. As Marie Delcourt points out, the actual presence of the abnormal formation of the reproductive organs in a living

---

* "She was of more than average size for a woman. Her breasts were meager, her hips narrow, the muscles of her arms, of course, were more powerfully developed than is usually the case in women, and her grasping hands, though not as big as a man's, were yet not so small either as to rule out the question whether she might not, Heaven forbid, be a boy in disguise. No, the female conformation of her breasts was unambiguous, and so too, despite her slenderness, the form of her thighs. She barely smiled. Her beautiful lips, far from being compressed, were usually slightly parted, but so were also, of course, in a tense way the nostrils of her Grecian nose."

person was the extreme of monstrosity to the Ancients, an ill omen, as evidenced by the fact that the new-born child bearing real or apparent signs of hermaphroditism was exposed and left to die.[1] It is only the representation of the hermaphrodite in art or in ritual that can function as a symbol of primordial unity.

Andromache's function, then, is strictly symbolic. Her startling incarnation of androgyny prompts Krull to ask whether she is human. While he thinks of her as an angel, she is more of a divinity. The fact that her element is the air – all of her feats are performed there, and never once is she depicted as resting on the earth – symbolizes her status as a heavenly goddess. Her features are severe and noble – a prefiguration of Senhora Kuckuck's stern and majestic countenance. She disdains all flirtatiousness toward the crowd. Her only form of recognition of the audience is a barely perceptible gesture of greeting with one hand, but her serious eyes stare straight ahead and do not join in the greeting. Coupled with her perpetual existence in the air, this lack of personal communication with the audience signifies her remoteness, her inaccessibility, and self-sufficiency. Her divine status is acknowledged by Krull when he confesses that he worshipped her. Her divine ambivalence is expressed when Krull experiences her vision as painful and uplifting at once. Painful perhaps, not only because she comes so startlingly close to a living embodiment of anatomical bisexuality, but also because her androgynous unity and the perfection of her artistry also symbolize her self-sufficiency and preclude her ability to love or to be loved. Krull surmises that sexual love is alien to her and that even as a mother she is unthinkable. Her libido is totally expended and lavished upon her art. Art as an alienator from life and from love – this persistent theme of Mann's works – is here translated into the mythical. Yet, Krull is tempted to imagine her as the beloved of Mustafa, the lion tamer. Seized by jealousy, he hastily banishes the thought.

Why this jealousy? The answer lies in Andromache's inaccessibility, her remoteness, her perfection and self-sufficiency, all of which threatens to diminish Krull's ego. At the same time, her image reactivates in Krull the primordial image of unity and the longing for this unity. But, paradoxically, Andromache herself cannot constitute the total fulfillment of this longing, since love is absent from her existence. Her unity is one of self-sufficient narcissism, and it is this unity together with her ambiguity of identity and her artistic existence which constitute her affinity with Krull. She is his alter ego. If Krull feels love for her, it is the result once again of narcissistic projection or transference.

What links the figure of Andromache to the pairs of brother and sister and of mother and daughter is this recurrent motif of the reactivation of the primordial image of unity which underscores the continuity of Krull's experience and symbolizes his longing for unity. As such, this experience is archetypal, which means also that it is universal and suprapersonal. The archetype, according to Jung, is an identical psychic structure common to all mankind and all ages, and is a product of the collective unconscious.

As a structural and thematic element of the work, the decisive functional significance of Krull's archetypal experiences lies in their capacity to form a bridge of transition from the personal to the suprapersonal and universal, from a highly cultivated ego-consciousness to the realm of the collective unconscious. Krull's experience of the archetypal world is the great catalyst in the formation of a new psychological conscience and new perspective on life and on mankind as a whole. Krull's psychological development gravitates toward a progressive inner humanization which presupposes the relinquishment of the egocentric and the narcissistic in favor of universally-oriented altruism. The frivolous guise of his behavior patterns is deceptive, for beneath it lies a profoundly serious psychological dialectic in which opposing forces struggle to become reconciled in a higher form of unity. This unity involves not only the harmonious union of *agape* and *eros* but also a union of the conscious with the unconscious, for Man's psychic wholeness, according to the Jungian therapeutic ideal, consists in the union of the conscious and the unconscious personality. For Krull, the experience of the archetype is the force which draws him into the orbit of the unconscious, a realm where the mythical and the psychological merge. Without this connection with the subterranean springs of man's being, Krull's existence draws nourishment only from the one-sidedness of individual consciousness in which man is only a fragment of his original self. Thus, as Mann's novel assumes more and more a mythic dimension, the motif of the unconscious must correspondingly become more prominent, and the attempt to enter it and to recover a lost unity becomes the psychic motivating force behind Krull's actions. The brother-sister pair, Andromache, and the mother-daughter pair are all variations on an archetypal symbol of unity. In their functional significance, these symbols not only point back to Man's primordial unity but also point forward to the goal to be reached. As archetypal symbols, they also mediate between the unconscious substratum and the conscious mind. Without them the conscious mind is split off from its origins.

It is characteristic of the archetype that the particular form and content it assumes in its symbolic embodiment derives from the particular nature of the individual consciousness that perceives it. Thus, the variations in actual form in these archetypal symbols correspond to stages in the psychology of Krull's ego development. The brother-sister pair reflects the immature, autoerotic level of self-contained and self-sufficient unity. Andromache represents the heavenly and remote goddess whose inaccessibility and self-sufficiency are symbolized in her hermaphroditic figure which also precludes sexual union. The inadequacy and incompleteness of the unity she presents is marked not only by the absence of love in her existence – and hence the impossibility of perceiving her as a mother symbol – but also by the ascetic withdrawal from society imposed upon her by the rigorous demands of her artistic existence. Her remoteness and separateness are a reflection of the loss of Krull's androgynous unity symbolized in the experience with Diane Philibert by the arousal of unequivocal male sexuality and the consciousness of his identity; as such, her symbol points back to a unity that has been lost, but also points ahead by activating a longing to recover this lost unity on a higher, more mature, and more inclusive level. The mother-daughter pair, finally, embodies the synthesis of youthful beauty and adult maturity. Not only that: it supplies the missing element of love and has the power of releasing Krull from excessive preoccupation with his own ego and of drawing him into its orbit. Senhora Kuckuck, as the mother, personifies the unconscious. By entering into her realm Krull submits his conscious ego-personality to the controlling influence of the unconscious. Before going into an elaborate discussion of the complex web of symbolism and symbolic action in this final episode, it will be helpful to consider the way in which Krull is psychologically prepared for this all-important contact with the mythical and with the representatives of the chthonian forces of the unconscious.

Aboard the train bound for Lisbon, Krull, now in the guise of Marquis de Venosta, reflects on the inner psychological changes that necessarily accompany his change of outward identity. First, he notes a profound sense of satisfaction deriving from the change and renewal of his worn-out self: "... die Veränderung und Erneuerung meines abgetragenen Ich überhaupt, daß ich den alten Adam hatte ausziehen und in einen anderen hatte schlüpfen können, dies eigentlich war es, was mich erfüllte und beglückte." (528)* The metaphor is interesting. The biblical Adam, as we have seen, may be considered a prototype of androgyny, since he carries Eve hidden within him. The most decisive psychological change, however, as Krull realizes, has to do with the continuity of inner existence – memory. In assuming a new outward identity he must also assume a new inner identity, which involves an emptying out of his inmost being: "Nur fiel mir auf, daß mit dem Existenzwechsel nicht allein köstliche Erfrischung, sondern auch eine gewisse Ausgeblasenheit meines Innern verbunden war, – insofern nämlich, als ich alle Erinnerungen, welche meinem ungültig gewordenen Dasein angehörten, aus meiner Seele zu verbannen hatte." (528)** For one so versed in the

---

* "What really filled me with happiness was the change and renewal of my worn-out self, the fact that I had been able to take off the old Adam and slip on a new."
** "I was struck, though, by the fact that with this change of identity there was connected not only a delightful refreshment but also a certain emptying out of my

secret powers of the will and the imagination as Krull, the question of the feasibility of such an operation is not even entertained. What *is* difficult, as Krull admits, is to replace his memories with other memories – those of Loulou, his alter ego – with any degree of precision. This leaves him with an inner emptiness, with a vagueness and confusion of memory. Apparently, Krull's amazing powers and talents are not quite equal to the requirements for a wholly successful memory transplant. Successful or not, Krull's efforts here amount to a tilling of the soil of his consciousness, a plowing deep enough to lay bare the subsoil of the unconscious which is being prepared for the the seeds of a new and richer crop of psychic experience.

Krull's unfinished odyssey as Marquis de Venosta may also be regarded as symbolic of a descent into the unconscious. Bound for Lisbon from Paris, his journey takes him "downward" along the earth's surface toward a region of great antiquity and of a racial mixture rich in variety and confusion. As he learns from Professor Kuckuck, Lisbon is also a city in which products of an older geological period of the earth's history are in evidence: "Aber mit eigenen Augen werden Sie Pflanzen dort sehen, die eigentlich gar nicht der gegenwärtigen Vegetation unseres Planeten angehören, sondern einer früheren, nämlich Farn-

innermost being, insofar as I had to banish from my soul all memories that belonged to my invalidated past."

bäume. Gehen Sie sogleich und sehen Sie sich die Baumfarne aus der Steinkohlenzeit an! Das ist mehr als kurzatmige Kulturgeschichte. Das ist Erdaltertum." (533)* The descent into a lower stratum of geological history symbolizes also his descent into a deeper layer of the psyche – the collective universal unconscious. Professor Kuckuck and his lectures on the universe and cultural history are psychologically preparatory experiences for Krull. Their effect is that of a tremendous expansion and alteration of Krull's consciousness. They are also important for their effect on Krull's ego, for relative to the vastness of the universe with its mysteries and amazing interrelatedness of phenomena man's ego must seem to him infinitesimal. These experiences all mark the beginning of a shift of consciousness from the egocentric to the infinitely larger concerns of the history of the universe and of humanity.

In the final part of the *Confessions*, then, the episode of dominant and elemental significance is Krull's relationship to the mother-daughter pair – Senhora Maria Pia and Zouzou Kuckuck. Mother and daughter form the structural and thematic counterpart to the phatasmagoric ap-

* "There you will see with your own eyes plants that actually do not belong to the present-day vegetation of our planet, but to an earlier one – I'm speaking here of the tree ferns. You must go without delay and have a look at the tree ferns of the Carboniferous period. That is more than just short-winded cultural history. That is geological time."

pearance of the brother-sister pair in the context of Krull's earlier experiences in Frankfurt. In the creation of the mother-daughter pair and its functional significance for Krull's development there can be little doubt that Mann utilized the core of the myth of Demeter and Persephone. That this myth, the central content of which is the biunity of mother and maiden daughter, possessed special significance for Mann is evident from the correspondence with Kerenyi. Here Mann tells how he was struck by the coincidence between his use of the motif of mother-daughter identity in *Joseph* (Mai-Sachme episode) and his later discovery on reading Kerenyi's *Das Ägyptische Fest* that the double-image of mother and daughter had a mythological precedent in the Demeter-Kore ritual of the Eleusinian Mysteries.[2]

Demeter (in Latin Ceres) was Goddess of the Corn. Her chief festival took place every five years in September, at harvest time, and lasted nine days. It consisted of processions, animal sacrifices, dancing, singing, and general rejoicing. The chief part of the ceremony, however, took place in the form of a worship at the great temple at Eleusis, a small town near Athens, whence the designation Eleusinian Mysteries. But since those visitors and initiates who witnessed this ceremony were bound by a vow of silence, posterity's knowledge of the actual content of the Mysteries is based on inference from scattered bits of information. The oldest literary account of the myth of Demeter and Persephone is the *Homeric*

THE ELEUSINIAN MYSTERIES REVISITED

Hymn to Demeter which appears to have as its object an explanation of the origin of the Eleusinian Mysteries. The poem relates how the youthful maiden, Persephone, was gathering flowers in a lush meadow. Enticed by the beguiling scent of the narcissus, she strayed too far from her companions. Pluto, lord of the Dead, rose from the abyss as the earth gaped, and abducted her in his golden chariot to the Underworld where she was to be his bride and queen. Demeter, the grieving mother, sought her daughter over land and sea. She wandered nine days before learning from the Sun of her daughter's fate. In her wrath at her bereavement she withheld grain from the earth, causing the land to become frozen and lifeless. She left Olympus, vowing never to return and never to allow the corn to sprout again until her lost daughter would be restored to her, and took up her abode at Eleusis. Finally, Zeus, realizing the intolerability of the famine on earth, decided to take the matter in hand. After sending by turns the gods to Demeter in an attempt to persuade her to turn from her anger and restore the fruits of the earth to Man, and seeing each of these attempts unsuccessful, he commissioned Hermes to descend into the Underworld and bring Persephone back to her mother. In short, Hermes carries out his task successfully, and Persephone is returned to her mother. After Demeter sees her daughter, she hastens to the kings of Eleusis to initiate them and to show them the sacred rites by which the event is to be solemnized. But Pluto had given Persephone a pomegranate seed to eat before her departure, knowing that this would cause her to return to him. This accounts for the stipulation by Zeus that henceforth Persephone should spend two-thirds of every year with her mother and the gods in the upper world and one-third of the year (the winter) with her husband in the nether region. Every year in spring Persephone returns to the earth and to her mother, which becomes an occasion for joy and the blossoming of flowers and vegetation.

A question arises as to what the actual core of the Eleusinian Mysteries might have been, for the myth, as it is recounted in the Homeric hymn, suggests little or nothing that could have been the source of awe and mystery. For my purpose here, it is sufficient to point out that the mystery, at least in part, has been interpreted as the identity and unity of mother and daughter.[3] This assumption is based on external evidence. In Greek art, the relief-portraits of mother and daughter are often so alike as to be scarcely distinguishable from one another.[4] In worhip they are given the official title "The Goddesses" which in ancient Greek is rendered not in the plural but in the old dual form, *tō theō*, which suggests a unity in duality. The two goddesses are thus worshipped as one. It is not their portraits so much as their attributes by which they are distinguishable. Persephone is the maiden by virtue of the flower she bears and Demeter is characterized as the mature goddess by the fruit.⁵ But in one famous relief, in which the two look smilingly into each other's eyes, both hold flowers, symbolizing their interchangeability. Finally, a stone inscription on Delos strongly suggests the identity of the two goddesses under still another aspect. It reads: "(Property) of Demeter the Eleusinian, maiden and woman."⁶ If interpreted correctly, the inscription bears testimony to the fact that "maiden" and "woman" were regarded as simultaneous attributes of the mother goddess. Taken as a whole, these indices speak decidedly in favor of the assumption that this mother-daughter biunity was of central significance in the Mysteries. They suggest that either the originally separate individualities of the two goddesses, mother and daughter, had virtually merged in a single divine figure or that the two goddesses may be regarded as different aspects of a single one.

This extensive summary of the myth of Demeter and Persephone provides us with a starting-point for determining the motifs Mann utilized in his composition of the mother-daughter episode. It is obvious, first of all, that the mother-daughter biunity, to which Krull refers with repeated and untiring enthusiasm, is given direct expression in the circumstance that the disparate charms of Zouzou and her mother blend into an enchanting image of complementary wholeness. In the pair Krull beholds beauty in a double image, as childlike blossom and regal maturity, which corresponds to the ancient image of the relationship between virgin daughter and mother as that of flower and fruit. Senhora Kuckuck and Zouzou are represented, then, as a double figure, one half of which is the ideal complement of the other. Secondly, what might be regarded as an ironic reversal of the archetypal situation lies in the circumstance that, while in the Homeric hymn it is Hermes who is entrusted with the mission of returning the abducted daughter to her mother, in Mann's treatment it is Krull-Hermes who plays the role of seducer and alienator. In the psychological adaptation of the myth the wily and protean Krull-Hermes demonstrates the Heraclitean *enantiodromia*, the tendency of a person or thing to turn into its diametrical opposite. But the role of Krull as seducer is also meaningful in a more straightforward way. In the matriarchal world of the Demeter myth and the Eleusinian Mysteries – a theme to which I shall return for elaboration later – the role of the male who comes from without is that of intruder, seducer, or conqueror.

While these specific motifs and situations may may be related to the Demeter myth in particular, the character of Senhora Kuckuck represents at the same time something still more universal and primordial – she is an embodiment of the archetype of the Great Mother. As Jung points out, mythology and the history of religion present several variations of the mother archetype, of which the mother who reappears as the maiden in the myth of Demeter and Kore is but one instance.[7] In the Cybele-Attis myth, for example, the mother is also the beloved.[8] There are other mother symbols in a figurative sense such as the Mother of God, the Virgin, and Sophia. That Mann has condensed these various symbols of the mother archetype in the figure of Senhora Kuckuck is apparent, first of all, from her name, Maria Pia da Cruz ('Holy Mary of the Cross'), with its unmistakable suggestion of the Virgin Mary. This makes her mother and virgin in one – another confirmation of the identity between mother and daughter. Secondly, since she is ultimately Krull's beloved, she becomes identifiable also with the Cybele-Attis myth.

As the embodiment of the archetype of the Great Mother (the term "great", according to Erich Neumann, expresses the symbolic character of superiority), Senhora Kuckuck personifies the unconscious in two distinct senses. First, to enter into her, i.e. into the womb, is to enter the prenatal realm of the unconscious and to be reborn. Secondly, she is the projected image of what Jung calls the *anima* in men, that representative of the unconscious which bears the imago ideal or soul-image of woman, of the Eternal Feminine.[9] The *anima* may be projected not only to the symbolic mother (Senhora Kuckuck), but also on to the daughter (Zouzou), the sister, the beloved, the heavenly goddess (Andromache), and the earth spirit Baubo (Rozsa and Diane-Hecate). It is this factor of projection on to various types of the Eternal Feminine that links together virtually all the female characters who figure significantly in Krull's emotional experiences. On to each of these figures is projected one particular aspect of Krull's *anima*; hence, each of these projections is also a reflection of the particular state of his emotional maturity, a key to the progress in his development toward mature, non-narcissistic love. Of these female figures, however, only Diane Philibert and Senhora Kuckuck qualify as mother symbols, though in quite different ways. Diane is a mother symbol only by virtue of her maternal solicitude, whereas Senhora Kuckuck embodies the Mother Archetype in a more inclusive sense. Unlike Diane, she is actually a mother and, more importantly, she is capable of true, unperverted love. But neither, interestingly enough, has a son.

On his very first encounter the mother-daughter pair becomes immediately linked in Krull's mind with the brother-sister pair. The archetypal image of aesthetic biunity in complementary pairs of persons is here reactivated and projected. In each case Krull's emotional experience reflects the *numinous* character of the personified archetype. It is characteristic of the archetypal symbol, according to Erich Neumann, that it grips the personality as a whole, arouses and fascinates it, draws the subject under its spell and compels the conscious mind to interpret it.[10] Neumann explains this dynamic effect of the archetype upon the ego as an expression of its superiority over the ego-consciousness.[11] By virtue of the tremendous attraction which the archetypal symbol exerts upon the psyche, the ego is easily overpowered.

As Krull himself remarks: "... ich will... hinzufügen, daß meine Faszination durch die sehr bald auftauchende Vermutung genährt wurde, daß hier der Zufall ein wunderliches Spiel treibe." (559)* Krull's consciousness is set in motion and strives to assimilate the symbol. In Zouzou he perceives a startling resemblance to Zaza which touches off a series of questions in his mind as to the reasons for his forming this connection and the emotional excitement attendant upon it: "Eine andere Zaza – so anders in der Tat, daß ich mich nachträglich frage, ob eine eigentliche Ähnlichkeit, wenn ich sie auch mit Augen zu sehen glaubte, überhaupt vorlag. Glaubte ich sie vielleicht nur zu sehen, weil ich sie sehen *wollte*, weil ich... nach einer Doppelgängerin Zaza's auf der Suche war? Ich bin über diesen Punkt nicht ganz mit mir im reinen. Sicherlich hatten in Paris meine Gefühle denjenigen des guten Loulou keinerlei Konkurrenz gemacht; ich war in seine Zaza, so gern sie mit mir geäugelt hatte, durchaus nicht verliebt gewesen. Kann es sein, daß ich die Verliebtheit in sie in meine neue Identität aufgenommen, daß ich mich nachträglich in sie verliebt hatte und in der Fremde einer Zaza zu begegnen wünschte?" (559)* Krull's specula-

* "... I want to add that my fascination received nourishment from the sudden suspicion that coincidence was playing here a remarkable game."
* "A different Zaza – so different, in fact, that I was obliged to ask myself afterward whether there was here a

THE ELEUSINIAN MYSTERIES REVISITED

tions are interesting, but they lead us astray rather than bringing us closer to an explanation. It is, after all, not Zaza with whom Krull is falling in love but Zouzou, the projection of his *anima*. But since, in Krull's experience, mother and daughter constitute a biunity, his projection is necessarily a double one, directed on to mother and daughter simultaneously. The best expression of this double projection is contained in the following response of Krull to Senhora Kuckuck's inquiry as to Krull's impressionability: "'... gleich mein erster Tag in Lissabon hat mir Eindrücke von Frauenschönheit beschert, die mich... gegen weitere recht unempfänglich machen.' Dabei küßte ich ihr die Hand, während ich gleichzeitig mit einem Lächeln zu Zouzou hinüberblickte. So handelte ich immer. Das Doppelbild wollte es so. Wenn ich der Tochter eine Artigkeit sagte, so sah ich nach der Mutter, und umgekehrt." (630)** In interpreting Krull's experiences of

real similarity even if I believed that I was seeing it with my own eyes. Did I perhaps believe I was seeing it because I *wanted* to see it, because I was in search of Zaza's double? I am not quite clear in my own mind on this point. To be sure, in Paris my emotions had not in any way competed with those of good Loulou; no matter how much she ogled with me, I was not at all in love with his Zaza. Can it be that I took up being in love with her as part of assuming a new identity, that I had fallen in love with her *post hoc* and was desirous of meeting a Zaza abroad?"

** "'On the very first day in Lisbon I was presented with impressions of feminine beauty that have made mother and daughter we must adapt ourselves to a peculiar kind of vision in which neither the figure of the mother nor the figure of the daughter is seen as a separate and distinct entity. Mother and daughter are one; each figure embodies simultaneously its complement.

The countenance of Senhora Kuckuck symbolizes the ambivalence of the primordial mother archetype which combines both positive and negative attributes.[12] The Great Mother is at once terrible and loving, frightening and attractive, destructive and creative. This is ultimately the ambivalence of the divinity, for Senhora Kuckuck also personifies Demeter, the mother goddess. It is the negative qualities of the Terrible Mother which Krull first perceives in her countenance: "Ein schwarzes, mit Silber ausgeziertes Sammetband, das ihren Hals umschloß, kleidete sie sehr wohl, wie auch die baumelnden Jettgehänge, und mochte zu dem Stolz ihrer Kopfhaltung beitragen, einer betonten Würde, die übrigens ihre ganze Erscheinung beherrschte und sich fast bis zur Düsternis, fast bis zur Härte in ihrem ziemlich großen Gesicht mit den hochmütig verpreßten Lippen, den gespannten Nüstern, den beiden gestrengen Furchen zwischen den Brauen malte. Es war die Härte des

me quite unreceptive to further ones.' At this I kissed her hand, smiling at the same time at Zouzou. This is the very way I always acted. The double image required it. When I paid the daughter a compliment, I looked at the mother, and vice versa."

Südens..." (561)* This terrifying severity, which on the surface is the dominant strain, can on occasion be counterbalanced by signs of affection: "Hoheitsvoll vermahnend, mit Kopfschütteln blickte die Senhora auf ihr Kind wegen dessen Heiterkeitsausbruchs – und konnte sich dann doch selbst eines Lächelns ihrer gestrengen Lippen nicht erwehren, auf deren oberer ein ganz schwacher Schatten von Schnurrbart dunkelte." (563)**

Such are Krull's initial impressions of mother and daughter. Since both represent the unconscious, Krull's progressive familiarization with the two signifies on the symbolic level his gradual initiation into the unconscious. As we have seen, this descent into both the unconscious and the dark past of man's existence is prepared for by other events of a symbolic nature. His initial encounter with mother and daughter takes place quite by accident at a sidewalk café. Between this introduction and his ensuing first visit at

* "A black velvet neckband trimmed with silver was very becoming to her, as were also her dangling jet earrings, and doubtless contributed to the note of pride in the carriage of her head. This dignity was pronounced and dominated furthermore her whole appearance. It was expressed almost to the point of somberness, almost to severity, in her rather large face with its haughty, compressed lips, tense nostrils, and the two severe creases between her brows. It was the sternness of the south."
** "The senhora glanced at her child, shaking her head in regal admonishment at this outburst of merriment – and then could not suppress a smile from her severe lips, of which the upper one was darkened by a very faint shadow of a moustache."

their home he is taken on a tour through Professor Kuckuck's Museum of Natural History which, as he says, he regarded "als Vorbereitung... zum Wiedersehen mit Mutter und Tochter, – ganz ähnlich, wie Kuckucks Gespräch im Speisewagen die Vorbereitung gewesen war zu dieser Besichtigung." (581)* The one feature of this tour with the greatest symbolical import is the descent into the museum basement to view lifelike exhibits depicting scenes from the early life of Man. This "descent" is strikingly reminiscent of the Prologue to the Joseph novels where Mann leads the reader on a downward journey into the deep well of the past. On another level, this web of symbolism connecting the descent into the primitive past with the descent into the chthonian unconscious sphere of the mother archetype is very suggestive of Faust's descent into the realm of 'The Mothers.' Mephistopheles' paradoxical command "Dein Wesen strebe nieder" ('Strive downward!') is parodied by Krull's corrective interpretation of this "descent" as actually an "ascent" in terms of Man's position on the evolutionary scale. In this same context there is another instance of reversal which is considerably less obvious but equally interesting. For his reunion with mother and daughter at the Kuckuck villa Krull must travel *upward* by cable car. Here the depths of the unconscious are

* "... as a preparation for the reunion with mother and daughter – just as Kuckuck's conversation in the dining-car had been a preparation for this inspection tour."

symbolized by their ironic opposite: height. As in the Joseph novels, the interchangeability of Above and Below is exploited to the utmost.

In Krull's second meeting with mother and daughter the ambivalent qualities of Senhora Maria Pia become intensified and the contrasts are brought out more sharply by a proliferation of symbols. The cozy atmosphere of the rooms of the house is offset by a feeling of timidity at the sight of the mother. The dynamic superiority of the Great Mother has the effect of relativizing the independence of Krull's ego-consciousness. Senhora Kuckuck now appears in a different attire: a dress of very fine snowy white moiré with a black silk sash worn under her bosom. The snowy whiteness of her dress is a symbol of virginity, of her identity with her daughter. But white is contrasted with black, the symbol of the dark forces of the unconscious and also of death. The ivory tint of her skin appears several shades darker against the whiteness of her dress, and a few threads of silver are discernible in her heavy dark hair. In pictorial and plastic representations of antiquity the Earth Mother is generally dark.[13] Her ambivalence is apparent in color symbolism. Her colors are red (symbol of life and blood) and black (the dark unconscious and death). In the description of Maria Pia this substitution of white for the archetypal red not only sustains the suggestion of ambivalence but also skillfully symbolizes the interchangeability of mother and daughter. Krull does not deny that this woman terrifies and attracts him at the same time. He feels that the forbidding majesty of her demeanor is somewhow connected with a property of blood, of racial arrogance and that it has an animal quality about it. The remark subtly hints at the subsequent bull sacrifice. In this connection, Maria Pia's "trembling earrings" – referred to repeatedly – may be interpreted as a symbol of animal sex instinct and procreation. It is neither far-fetched nor irreverent to see them as representations of the dangling testes of the bull. As Erich Neumann points out, "the aggressive and destructive features of the Great Mother... can be distinguished as masculine, and among her attributes we also find phallic symbols."[14] The habitual presence and reference to this phallic symbol not only corresponds to Demeter's capacity as fertility goddess but also signifies the unity of childbearing and begetting, of life and death. It underscores the idea of ambivalence and bisexuality.

The bullfight leads with mounting excitement to the grand climax of the work. It is a sombre celebration, infused with a great profundity and richness of symbolism in which many mythical motifs and levels of cultural history are condensed. For Krull it is an experience which alters his attitude toward the double image. It reverses the emphasis, he says, "indem es den einen Teil, den mütterlichen, mit sehr starkem Licht, einem blutroten, übergoß und den anderen, den reizend töchterlichen, dadurch ein wenig in den Schatten stellte." (645)* The Great Mother reverts here to her original colors of red and black (life and love versus death, creation versus destruction). Because of the dominant role that Senhora Kuckuck (Demeter) assumes in this episode and her apparently mysterious relationship to the events taking place in connection with the bullfight, the whole festive occasion may be interpreted as *her* festival and hence identified with the ancient Eleusinian Mysteries which Demeter is said to have initiated. As pointed out earlier, Demeter's festival was held every five years at harvest time in September. Krull's visit to the bullfight takes place in late September. His emotional reaction to the sight of the festive crowd and of the arena is essentially the same as his archetypal experiences of the double image. There is, in his own words, "... etwas Dumpfes, Urtümliches darin, das zwar jene Ehrfurcht, aber auch etwas Sorge erregt." (648)** The remark attests to the typical ambivalence that the archetypal image calls forth.

The Eleusinian Mysteries and the psychology of the Demeter cult bear characteristics of a matriarchal order of society.[15] The matriarchal stage in the development of culture is the phase in

* "... by placing the one aspect, the mother, in a very strong light, flooding it, in fact, with a light that was blood-red in color, and putting the other aspect, the enchanting daughter, a little in the shade."
** "... something inarticulate, primordial about it that arouses awe, to be sure, but also a certain anxiousness."

which the Feminine is preponderant over the Masculine or, on the symbolic level, the unconscious is superior to ego-consciousness.[16] Krull's feeling of timidity in the presence of the stern mother is symptomatic of the power of the archetypal feminine to relativize independence. It indicates that the power of the unconscious has become dominant over the ego and consciousness. It is the overpowering force of the elemental character of the Feminine to which this must be attributed. A careful examination of the relationships that prevail in the Kuckuck family reveals the survival of the matriarchal structure. Apart from Krull, the male characters – Hurtado and Professor Kuckuck – play decidedly passive roles. Hurtado's function in the company of mother and daughter is the subordinate one of male escort without whom the females, as Krull notes, would not, according to the customs of the country, have been allowed to appear in certain public places. Professor Kuckuck seems anything but a patriarchal figure. In the family circle his presence is marked by benevolent inattention and absentminded kindliness. The most telling characterization of his subordinate role is contained in Krull's remark: "Wenn ich der Tochter eine Artigkeit sagte, so sah ich nach der Mutter, und umgekehrt. Die Sternenaugen des Hausherrn zuoberst der kleinen Tafel blickten auf diese Vorkommnisse mit vagem Wohlwollen, dem Erzeugnis der Siriusferne, aus der sein Zuschauen kam. Die Ehrerbietung, die ich für ihn empfand, litt nicht

THE ELEUSINIAN MYSTERIES REVISITED

den geringsten Schaden durch die Wahrnehmung, daß sich bei meinem Werben um das Doppelbild jede Rücksicht auf ihn erübrigte." (630)* There is not a single instance in which Professor Kuckuck acts with the strict authority of a *paterfamilias*, neither as a decision-maker nor as an overseer. It is not he but the mother who plays the role of a stern moral guardian over the social and sexual welfare of her daughter. Erich Neumann's interpretation of the close connection between mother and daughter in the Eleusinian Mysteries may be validly applied to the relationship obtaining between Senhora Kuckuck and her daughter. This close connection, according to Neumann, has to do with "the preservation of the primordial relationship between them. In the eyes of the female group, the male is an alien, who comes from without and by violence takes the daughter from the mother."[17] Perhaps the best testimony to the commanding role of Senhora Kuckuck is the timid silence hanging over the coach ride to the festival. Krull remarks: "Die Fahrt verging in einer Schweigsamkeit oder doch Spärlichkeit des Austausches, die hauptsächlich von Senhora Maria's außergewöhnlich würdevoller, ja starrer

---

* "When I paid the daughter a compliment, I looked at the mother, and vice versa. The starry-eyed man of the house at the head of the small table looked upon these gestures with vague benevolence, a testimony of the stellar distances from which he gazed. The reverence I felt for him was not in the slightest impaired by the realization that in my wooing of the double image any consideration for him was superfluous."

und kein Geplauder aufkommen lassender Haltung bestimmt wurde." (649)*

The killing of the bull symbolizes the blood sacrifice demanded by the goddess of fertility.[18] Just as the fertile years of the female demand, in a symbolic sense, the sacrifice of blood in menstruation, the breaking of the hymen, and the loss of virginity, and finally in the act of giving birth, so also does the fertility ritual of the Great Mother, the bestower of all nourishment, demand the flow of blood, the life sap, from the sacrificial offering to fecundate the earth (a female symbol) and to renew its fertility. In demanding this sacrifice the Great Mother reveals herself once again in her dual aspect as both the giver and taker of life, as both creative and destructive. In this capacity she is identical with the bull who, in his elemental ferocity, is the theriomorphic symbol of both a procreative and murderous force. By virtue of this union of opposites the bull is also the symbol of a divinity, a god-animal or an animal god. Krull observes during the course of the sacrifice that the event has cast Dona Maria Pia completely under its spell. Her intense excitement is manifested in the surging of her bosom, and he surmises that the stern and elemental person of this woman is inextricably bound up with the game of blood below. The key to the

* "The ride passed in silence or with very little exchange of words, which was due mainly to Senhora Maria's unusually dignified, indeed, rigid, demeanor, which tolerated no chitchat."

meaning of this mysterious connection lies in a complicated web of symbolism, the disentangling of which requires our reading the events on two different levels of cultural history which Mann has here skillfully merged into one: the matriarchal world of the Eleusinian Mysteries and the patriarchal culture of Mithraism.

In his learned commentary on the events Krull witnesses, Professor Kuckuck speaks of "einem uralten römischen Heiligtum, wo es aus dem Oberen, Christlichen, tief hinabgehe in die Kultschicht einer dem Blut sehr geneigten Gottheit, deren Dienst einst um ein Haar demjenigen des Herrn Jesu den Rang als Weltreligion abgelaufen hätte..." (656)* That ancient Roman shrine is the cult of Mithras, the ancient Persian god of light, defender of truth, and enemy of the powers of darkness. Mithraism was the religion of the Roman legionaries and admitted only men as initiates.[19] The Mithraic sacrifice is thus not only embedded in the context of a later patriarchal world which superseded the matriarchal culture, but its deity also represents those forces – light, truth, hostility toward darkness – which stand in diametrical opposition to what the Great Mother symbolizes: the dark and irrational forces of the unconscious. Professor Kuckuck interprets the events connected

* "... a very ancient Roman shrine which had descended from the high level of Christianity to the very deep stratum of service to a deity well disposed toward blood; the worship of this deity at one time almost came to outranking that of the Lord Jesus as a world religion."

with the bull sacrifice in terms of the paternal principle of Logos, of rationality and consciousness. But it is possible and, indeed necessary, to interpret the symbolic meaning of the bull sacrifice on the two levels even though each represents a force which is the antithesis of the other. This dual interpretation is warrented not only by the syncretistic nature of the historical development of religion and myth, but also because the synthesis toward which the opposing forces in Krull's personality struggle is that of the maternal unconscious and Eros and the paternal consciousness and Logos. The meaning underlying the symbolism of the blood-sacrifice is thus the same principle of unity in duality which is virtually the central theme of the *Confessions*.

The archetypal role of the father, as representative of intellect and reason, is to oppose pure animal instinctuality. Thus the killing of the bull, on the Mithraic level, symbolizes the overcoming of animal instinct.[20] Man's animal instinctuality (symbolized by the bull) must be sacrificed. On the earlier matriarchal level, however, the killing of the bull is a sacrifice to the Great and Terrible Mother and hence to the unconscious. In a very broad sense, then, not only the bull, but also the conscious mind is sacrificed to the unconscious. The sacrifice, in the matriarchal context, is a symbol of consciousness relinquishing its power and submitting itself to the forces of the unconscious. This becomes a prerequisite for the eventual synthesis of the maternal and paternal principles. The surging of Senhora Kuckuck's bosom has a sexual meaning on two levels. Both have to do with the fact that in the fertility ritual sexuality and nourishment are related (the emphasis on Maria Pia's breast connects also with the nourishment motif). Hence the sacrifice is also a fertilization of the mother. The blood from the sacrificed animal drops to the earth (a mother symbol) and impregnates it to insure fruit and grain for the new agricultural year. This is the motif of renewal which plays a prominent part in blood sacrifice.[21] On another level, the excitement of Senhora Kuckuck anticipates the quest hero's (i.e., Krull's) re-entry into the womb and consequent rebirth. Neumann points out that ritual killing provides the necessary transition toward both new fertility and rebirth.[22] In the final section of this analysis I shall return to this motif of the rebirth of the quest hero for an elaboration of its significance. For the present, it is sufficient to see this act as an adumbration of the final goal toward which the novel moves: the union of the conscious and the unconscious.

We must now turn to a consideration of the role of Zouzou whom our analysis has neglected so far and who also, as Krull himself says, had disappeared completely from his mind during the game of blood. As Persephone, Zouzou is, of course, always implicit in the figure of her mother, since, as we have seen, the central content of the Eleusinian Mysteries is the identity of mother and maiden daughter. In general, however, Mann's portrait of Zouzou represents his freest treatment in the adaptation of the Demeter-Persephone myth. Her childish forthrightness of expression, a reflection of her dictum that "silence is unhealthy," indicates that Mann is more inventive in his portrait of her, adding interesting psychological idiosyncracies to the mythic and collective elements.

Zouzou's central function is that she constitutes the object of Krull's amourous pursuit and seduction. Krull's love for her is ostensibly the result of his assumption of Venosta's identity and also of his perceiving in her Zaza's double. The reader is thus induced to believe that Krull, in assuming Venosta's social identity, also received the Marquis' libido and *anima* as well. It is highly doubtful, however, that our credulity can be exploited to such an extent. Krull's love is the result of a psychological development and does not have a mystical explanation. Exposed to the influences of archetypal experiences and to the forces of the collective unconscious, the narcissism of his ego-consciousness gradually yields to the dynamics of heterosexual love. With the reduced importance attached to the self, the conditions are present for a flowing over of ego-libido on to the object. The fact that Krull's love for Zouzou seems and probably *is* immature does not preclude the decisive psychic conversion from ego-idealization to object-idealization. But as Senhora Kuckuck puts it: "Youth is generally too young for youth."

THE ELEUSINIAN MYSTERIES REVISITED

In this sense her reproach of Krull's attempts at seduction as childish and immature, since they are directed toward a child rather than toward a mature woman, is particularly illuminating.

Krull's pursuit of Zouzou and the resistance he encounters in her caustic and disarming parries recalls the mythological motif of the male pursuit of the reluctant goddess. Pursued by the god's desire, the goddess transforms herself into various forms of unapproachable wild beasts or, as in the case of Daphne pursued by Apollo, into a tree. Krull's repeated reference to Zouzou as a thorny personality suggests her transformation into a briar. In myth the reluctant goddess is generally unreceptive to entreaty and is not to be softened by love. As for the motifs of abduction and separation, which play such a central role in the myth of Demeter and Persephone, we detect in Mann's treatment both a parallel and an ironic reversal. Krull admits that his goal is to seduce Zouzou, even though this objective is beset with formidable obstacles, not only in the circumstance that Zouzou is generally either heavily chaperoned or in the presence of companions, but also in her own headstrong resistance to love and in her ascetic notion of its impropriety and unhygienic character. In Mann's adaptation, seduction amounts to conquest rather than abduction, an overpowering of Zouzou's resistance and frigidity by the Hermetic art of verbal persuasion. Krull-Hermes succeeds in softening the reluctant Zouzou by his long discourse on the origin of Love which in many respects recalls Aristophanes' account in Plato's *Symposium* of the derivation of Man's sex drive from his longing to be reunited with the other lost half of his original hermaphroditic state (motif of separation and the longing to recover lost unity).

In the *Homeric Hymn to Demeter* Persephone was abducted by Pluto because she had strayed too far away from her companions while picking flowers in a lush meadow. She was beguiled, as the story runs, by heavily scented and stupefying flowers, particularly the narcissus. The locale for Krull's "seduction" is also idyllic. It is the rear garden of the Kuckuck residence to which Krull returns during the hour of Dona Maria Pia's siesta. Dahlias and asters bloom in the middle of the small lawn. Although this conquest does not result in actual abduction or sexual union, it does symbolize, in the eyes of Zouzou's mother, the threat of separation, of the disintegration of order and rational planning. The sudden appearance of the stern and wrathful mother at the very moment when estrangement is most imminent constitutes a radical departure from the myth. Mature reason and matronly foresight intervene at the crucial moment to preserve institutional solidarity. The motif of Demeter's grief over separation and the long search for her daughter, symbolizing the search for the lost half of herself, is compressed in Mann's treatment into a single, brief incident. Senhora Kuckuck does not have far or long to search. We do not know what prompts her to interrupt her siesta and to go to the garden, but we can surmise that it is the certainty of her instinct, the superiority of the unconscious of which she is the symbol. Senhora Kuckuck searches and finds Zouzou in the arms of Krull-Hermes. The mother goddess regains her daughter and therefore her lost unity. This "finding again" symbolizes the restoration of the matriarchal unity of mother and daughter which had been threatened by the incursion of the seducer into the matriarchal world.

Krull's passionate embrace of the primordial mother – the final and climactic scene of the novel – is polyvalent in its symbolism. On one level it significantly reiterates the motif of the unity and identity of mother and daughter. Since both are symbolically one and the same, their experiences may be duplicated. What happens to the daughter, happens also to the mother, and vice versa. In being "seduced" by Krull, Maria Pia experiences her daughter's seduction, and what is more – she "becomes" her daughter once again through the experience. This turn of events does not constitute a radical departure from the original myth, for, according to legend, Demeter is said to have been seduced by Poseidon while searching for her lost daughter.[23] The doubling of the motif thus confirms the identity or interchangeability of the two goddesses. On a second level, and from a psychoanalytical point of view, Krull's attempt to conquer the youthful Zouzou is an act of immaturity. Desirous of approaching Zouzou-Persephone, he finds Demeter, the mature half of the biunity, to be the more accessible one. Love and union grounded in maturity ultimately proves superior to the fatuous striving for conquest of the immature child, which, psychoanalytically interpreted, constitutes a reversion to narcissism, for the pursuit of sexual conquest, merely for the sake of conquest, derives from the need to replenish the ego.

On a third and more inclusive level, the union with the Great Mother symbolizes Krull's attainment of psychic wholeness through a union of the conscious and the unconscious, a synthesis of the paternal principle of light with the maternal powers of darkness. This conclusion is related to the mythological phase of the rebirth of the hero through entry into the mother's womb and should not be construed psychoanalytically as an infantile regression to the womb to regain the lost security of the prenatal uterine paradise. It is not the recovery of lost security but of lost unity on a higher plane that constitutes the climax of Krull's development. Krull's conquest of the Great Mother is comparable to Oedipus' victory over the Sphinx. In Erich Neumann's interpretation, Oedipus' incest and his vanquishing of the Sphinx are identical, two sides of the same process.[24] Krull conquers his terror of the Great Mother, enters into her womb and thereby overcomes the peril of the unconscious. This triumphant symbolical marriage and incest with the Great Mother is the expression of equilibrium and wholeness.

In addition, there is a vitally important humanizing aspect of this union. Speaking of the hero myth in general, Erich Neumann's characterization of its end phase may apply equally well to Krull: "The hero is not only conqueror of the mother; he also kills her terrible female aspect so as to liberate the fruitful and bountiful aspect."[25]

Krull's rebirth is the symbolical expression of regaining the primordial unity of Man on a higher, more mature, and more complete level. Krull's original unity, symbolized by his androgyny, is a pseudo-wholeness. It is an external unity without a complementary inner unity. His earlier personality, schismatic and self-centered, is dominated by narcissistic ego-consciousness and intellectual censorhip which give rise to a markedly ambivalent attitude toward societal relationships and preclude any sense of identification with collective or suprapersonal causes. Psychic wholeness, in Jung's words, "is never comprised within the compass of the conscious mind – it includes the indefinite and indefinable extent of the unconscious as well."[26] In Krull's archetypal experiences the contents of the collective unconscious burst in upon a highly cultivated autoerotic ego-consciousness, overpowering at first until they become assimilated by the conscious mind to make up a balanced psyche. Psychic maturity consists not in avoiding or fearing the irrationality of instinct and the supremacy of the unconscious but by exposing oneself to their influence. The unconscious is not merely the seat of dark and irrational forces but also the wellspring of creativity, the source of archetypal contents which have the power to expand and to humanize the conscious mind. Recognition of this fact is a prerequisite for attaining both psychic maturity and psychic liberation.

VII. MERCURIUS, ALCHEMY, AND THE UNION OF OPPOSITES

"'Hermetik' ist gut gesagt, Herr Naphta. 'Hermetisch' – das Wort hat mir immer gefallen. Es ist ein richtiges Zauberwort mit unbestimmt weitläufigen Assoziationen." (III, 706)* These words, needless to say, are those of Hans Castorp in one of his conversations on the Magic Mountain. And the discussion, of course, does not involve mythology but rather the alchemical and magical teachings of the fabled author Hermes Trismegistus. In mentioning the wealth of associations connected with hermetics Castorp is undoubtedly a spokesman for Thomas Mann and his richly associative thinking. This oblique autobiographical revelation is significant because it indicates a pattern of association between the classical Hermes and the world of alchemy which existed already in the early 1920's and which over the next two decades must surely have increased in polyvalent significance in view of the increasingly dominant role of myth in Mann's work. But while Hans Castorp goes on to mention that the word "hermetics" calls to his mind the hermetically sealed canning jar and its association with "conserving" and "being shut off from time," we must assume that Mann's range of association far transcended this homespun example. What, indeed, was the nature of Mann's associations with "hermetics" and what particular significance did this wealth of implication have for him? It will be very

* "'Hermetics' is well put, Herr Naphta. I've always liked the word 'hermetic.' It is a magic word with many vague and far-reaching associations."

instructive to pursue this question, first with particular reference to the theme of *Felix Krull* and, secondly, in connection with Mann's style or use of language.

Jung was struck by what he perceived to be parallels between the image patterns of alchemy in medieval Hermetic philosophy and his own psychology of individuation and transformation. The whole alchemical procedure from the beginning of the *opus* to the end was, in his view, symbolic, and these symbols were projections of the archetypes of the Collective Unconscious. The alchemist's search for the secret *lapis philosophorum* (Philosophers' Stone), by which base metals or substances could be transmuted into gold, reflects on a symbolical plane their projection of the mystery of psychic transformation into matter, their insight, in other words, into the need to transform the personality through a marriage or *conjunctio* of the male and female principles – of the conscious and the unconscious. Jung's attempt to connect his own archetypal psychology with earlier alchemical forms of thought is as ingenious as it is controversial. While it is totally irrelevant for our concerns here to entertain the question of its validity, it will be revealing to consider those aspects of Jung's symbolic interpretation of the alchemical process which can be significantly related to *Felix Krull*.

On the archetypal-symbolic level Jung interprets this union as an alchemical marriage or *conjunctio*.[1] The *conjunctio* takes place in the

MERCURIUS, ALCHEMY, AND THE UNION OF OPPOSITES

alchemical retort and requires a medium for its realization. This medium or mediator is Mercurius (mercury or quicksilver) named after the Roman counterpart to Hermes. Mercurius is not only the medium for the *conjunctio* but also, in the Jungian interpretation, "that which is to be united, since he is the essence or 'seminal matter' of both man and woman."[2] Mercurius is, in other words, hermaphroditic. For the genesis of this complex of ideas Jung cites the "philosophical explanation" of the natural philosopher Dorn in the latter's *Physica Trismegisti*:

> In the beginning God created *one* world (unus Mundus). This he divided into two – heaven and earth. Beneath this spiritual and corporeal binarius lieth hid a third thing, which is the bond of holy matrimony. This same is the medium enduring until now in all things, partaking of both their extremes. Without it they cannot be at all, nor they without this medium be what they are, one thing out of three.[3]

Jung then superimposes his own interpretation on to the alchemical account: "The division into two was necessary in order to bring the 'one' world out of the state of potentiality into reality. Reality consists of a multiplicity of things. But one is not a number; the first number is two, and with it multiplicity and reality begin."[4] Jung concludes that the alchemists saw in the evasive Mercurius this *unus mundus*, the original hermaphroditic unity of the world or of Being. Thus the alchemical *mysterium conjunctionis* is, in Jung's interpretation, "nothing less than a restoration of the original state of the cosmos."[5]

For Jung, then, the role of Mercurius as mediator in the *conjunctio* is a factor of central importance in the alchemical procedure. We must now consider the characteristics of Mercurius by virtue of which he came to assume such an all-important status in Hermetic philosophy. In alchemical writings "Mercurius" denotes not only the chemical element mercury or quicksilver, but also Mercury (Hermes) the god, Mercury the planet, and the secret transforming substance. Since he is hermaphroditic, Mercurius encompasses within himself numerous opposites and is, at the same time, their uniting symbol.[6] This is most clearly exemplified in his capacity as quicksilver. Both fluid and volatile, quicksilver unites within itself the contrary elements of water and fire. In alchemical parlance quicksilver was called "dry water" or, more popularly: "the water that does not make the hands wet."[7] For the alchemists, quicksilver was an indefinable, fascinating, irritating, paradoxical, and elusive element, the object of much puzzled speculation.[8] For in quicksilver they were presented with a liquid metal which had the capacity to dissolve gold and also to regenerate it. Like Hermes, Mercurius is versatile, changeable, and deceitful. One of his popular epithets is *versipellis* ('changing the skin, shifty').[9] At times he could be helpful to the alchemists, but at other times he was the elusive trickster and source of exasperation. By derivation from his capacity as quicksilver Mercurius comes to be both metallic and liquid, material and spiritual, cold and fiery, poison and healing.

The alchemists make repeated reference to the fact that the *opus*, i.e. the alchemical process, proceeds from the one and leads back to the one.[10] The procedure is thus circular and is symbolized by the *ouroboros*, the dragon devouring its own tail. As mediator, Mercurius comes to be identified with this self-devouring dragon which eventually consumes itself and dies in order to be reborn as the philosophers' stone. Even as dragon, Jung points out, Mercurius symbolizes the union of opposites: the chthonic earthly principle of the lowly serpent and the aerial principle of the bird.[11] Mercurius is the process by which the lowly and the material is transmuted into the higher and the spiritual. In the crude form of the *prima materia* he corresponds to the lowly beginning of the work. The *prima materia* is hermaphroditic, containing all metals and all colors, and capable of engendering itself. As mediator Mercurius is the process which transpires between the beginning and the end of the work; he is also the means by which the ultimate goal of *conjunctio* is effected. Finally, because of his androgynous or bisexual form, he is identical with the *conjunctio*. Mercurius thus stands at both the beginning and the end of the work. In the crude form of the *prima materia* he represents the original primordial Man disseminated throughout the physical world, and in his transsubstantiated form he represents the reconstituted unity and totality on a higher plane.

The parallelism in theme and motif between this Jungian account and the development of character and theme in *Felix Krull* is both striking and far-reaching. The hermaphroditic Mercurius, which recalls the mythologem of the primal bisexual Hermes, may be connected with the androgyny suggested in Krull's portrait. Like mercury or quicksilver, Krull's character is elusive and resists definitive classification and just as quicksilver was the object of much puzzled speculation on the part of the alchemists, so also do Krull's character and appearance present something of an enigma to his environment, frequently eliciting both fascination and vexation. Krull is no less shifty and versatile than Mercurius. The facility with which he assumes multifarious roles attests to his protean nature.

Even more impressive are the parallels in thematic development and motif. Krull's development recapitulates in highly refracted form the stages of the alchemical process. In his shabby beggar's clothing in which he first presents himself at the Hotel Saint James and Albany to begin his career he corresponds to Mercurius in the crude form of the *prima materia*, the base substance which stands for the lowly beginning of the work. The *prima materia*, as we have seen, is hermaphroditic, contains all metals and colors, and is a potentially transmuting substance. Krull is androgynous, universal in his endowments, and possessed of every potentiality. His period of service as elevator operator symbolizes both his capacity as "mediator" between Above and Below and the ambiguity of his status which hovers and vacillates between the heights and depths of social existence. After this prelude, which plays on both the ambiguity and potentiality of Krull's existence and development, his "promotion" to food scraper and scullery work constitutes a comedown in status and the absolute nadir of his development, the "lowly beginning," comparable to Joseph's abode in the pit. The process in which Krull is here involved is one of "restoration," a veritable travesty of the alchemical procedure, as suggested by his own characterization of the work: "Übrigens reichten meine Aufgaben bis in die Spülküche hinein, wo das Service, von Hand zu Hand gehend, eine Folge von Waschungen durchlief, um bei den Abtrocknern zu landen, zu denen ich mich zeitweise, angetan mit einer weißen Schürze, gesellt fand. So stand ich gleichsam am Anfang und am Ende der Wiederherstellungsprozedur." (469)* The ultimate goal of the *conjunctio* in Jung's symbolic interpretation of the alchemical *opus* involves both a transsubstantia-

* "My chores extended into the scullery, where the china was passed from hand to hand through a series of washings and ended up with the driers whom I found myself joining, from time to time, attired in a white apron. Thus, I stood, as it were, at the beginning and at the end of this process of restoration."

tion and a restoration of unity and totality on a higher plane. Both motifs figure in Krull's development. His assumption of Venosta's identity constitutes a transmutation on the social plane which prefigures the ultimate psychic transsubstantiation and symbolical rebirth through the *conjunctio*, the *hieros gamos*, with the Great Mother. In becoming Marquis de Venosta, appearance and social legitimation are added to the potential of noble substance, and in Senhora Kuckuck's embrace the end stage of transmutation is reached: the achievement of psychic wholeness through a union of the conscious and the unconscious.

Krull's development thus conforms in its essential aspects to both the mythical and the Jungian-psychoanalytical accounts of the Primordial Hermaphroditic Man in which archetypal patterns of Hermes and Mercurius merge. Krull may be identified on the symbolical level with the original hermaphrodite who in the process of individuation, which accompanies creation and the dawning of consciousness, splits into the classical brother-sister duality (Hermes and Aphrodite). Thus dissociated, he becomes the quest hero whose longing for a reconstitution of this union is reactivated by a series of experiences all of which are archetypal variants of a primordial unity. The regaining of this lost unity takes place in the *conjunctio* which signifies, at the same time, a unity on a higher plane by the achievement of psychic wholeness.

VIII. THE DIALECTIC OF THE HERMETIC STYLE

If it is true that style is part of the *total meaning* of the work of art, then, strictly speaking, our understanding and appreciation of both author and work remain incomplete until we define the functionality of his use of language and its analogical correspondence to the theme of the work. This correspondence between style and subject is precisely what I wish to demonstrate in this final chapter. My focus will be essentially on how one of the dominant themes of *Felix Krull* − striving for synthesis and unity in duality − is symbolically represented in the very details of Mann's use of language.

Paradoxically, the unity of Thomas Mann's style resides in its duality. If *Felix Krull,* in view of its long genesis, is any index of Mann's stylistic development over the years, then this development may be described as a progressive striving for a unity in duality. This persistently recurrent duality manifests itself not only in a variety of syntactical patterns such as concessive-qualifying clauses and the oxymoron (the collocation of antitheses), but also in the very tenor of his elaborately wrought and arduous sentences which is split between that of a lyrical panegyric and a scientific treatise, between intense emotional involvement and both rational coolness and Apollinian distance, the same basic ambitendency which characterizes Krull's own style of social interaction and of meeting experience in general. In the early essay "Bilse und Ich" (1906) Mann makes a statement which, I think, exposes the intellectual and aesthetic roots of this dualistic tenor of style: "Und ist nicht der strenge Bogen so gut wie die süße Leier ein apollinisches Werkzeug?... Nichts unkünstlerischer als der Irrtum, daß Kälte und Leidenschaft einander ausschlössen!" (X, 21)* Coolness and passion – these are basically Hermetic contraries, the union of water and fire in Mercurius as quicksilver. Not only that: in reading Walter F. Otto's *Die Götter Griechenlands* (1929) Mann learned, if he had not already known it, that in classical Greece a kinship was felt between the bow and the lyre and that Heraclitus saw in their similarity of outward form a symbol for the harmony of opposites. "Both," says Otto, "are strung with animal sinews. The same verb which is used for striking the strings of a musical instrument (psallo) is frequently applied to the snapping touch of the bowstring."[1] While the bow is inseparably linked with Apollo, it was Hermes who, according to the classical myth, invented the lyre and gave it to Apollo as a gift. In view of these symbolical and mythic associations attaching to the bow and the lyre, it is inevitable that we associate this pair of instruments in turn with the combination of the arrow and the lyre which Thomas Mann chose to be the emblem adorning the covers of his published works.[2]

In another essay, "Erziehung zur Sprache"

---

* "And is not the strict bow as well as the sweet lyre an Apollinian instrument?... There is nothing more alien to art than the mistaken notion that coolness and passion are mutually exclusive."

(1920), we find echoed this same basic idea of a fusion of passionate involvement and objective detachment. In the context of how the pedagogue should teach style, Mann pleads for dispelling what he calls "das nationale Vorurteil" ("the national prejudice") which views objectivity and beauty as mutually exclusive.[3] What emerges as the common denominator of these pronouncements is the preoccupation with the idea of a synthesis of elements which conventionally are regarded as polar antitheses. For Thomas Mann, such diametrical opposites as passion and reason or, more specifically, the spontaneous and impassioned speech of lyric poetry and the cool, analytical, and intellectually penetrating style of the scientist or critic are not incompatible or irreconcilable. Statements indicative of a tendency toward synthesis are consistently encountered in Mann's essays. In "Der alte Fontane" (1910) Mann admires the coexistence of both conservative and revolutionary views in Fontane.[4] In "Tischrede auf Pfitzner" (1919) he admits that the notions of Romanticism and revolution may be thought of as antitheses, but insists that they are in no way organically contrary to each other.[5] Similarly, in *Doktor Faustus* Adrian Leverkühn advocates a new style of music in which the archaic is combined with the revolutionary. Collectively, these statements are testimony to the effect that synthesis is a stylistic as well as an intellectual concern of Thomas Mann. If, for example, we see Mann's penchant for parody – to cite one large aspect of his style – as a medium for the artistic realization of the synthesis of poetry and intellectualism, of lyric and logic, passion and reason, subjectivity and objectivity, spontaneity and artifice, and of conservatism and progressivism, we are better able to understand and appreciate that parody and its attendant duality of tenor is inherent in Mann's style almost from the beginning of his creativity to the very end. But precisely because parody so utterly pervades Mann's style, it can never be subjected to an exhaustive analysis. Instead, I shall be content, for the present, with citing an outstanding example of the kind of pervasive duality I have been talking about in which the tenor of the style is marked by the intermingling of lyrical and rational elements. In this passage Krull describes his experience of riding with Rozsa in a coach to her apartment. It is an erotic situation with romantic overtones. Krull's emotional experience is reproduced in a tone of urgency which is counterbalanced and ultimately smothered under the weight of heavily abstract and analytical language:

> Erst jetzt, da das Nachtgefährt sich wieder in trottendes Rollen gesetzt hatte, begann unser Gespräch... *Es entbehrte der Einleitung,* dieses Gespräch, *es entbehrte jeder höflichen Umständlichkeit;*[6] *von allem Anfang an* und *durchaus* eigenete ihm die *unbedingte, enthobene* und *entbundene Unverantwortlichkeit,* die sonst nur dem Traum eigentümlich ist, wo unser Ich mit

THE DIALECTIC OF THE HERMETIC STYLE

Schatten ohne gültiges Eigenleben, mit Erzeugnissen seiner selbst verkehrt, wie sie jedoch im wachen Dasein, worin ein Fleisch und Blut wirklich getrennt gegen das andere steht, eigentlich nicht stattfinden kann. Hier fand sie statt, und gern gestehe ich, daß ich in *tiefster* Seele angesprochen war von der *berauschenden Seltsamkeit des Vorkommnisses.* (380)*

What Krull wants to communicate to the reader is the singularity of the situation, an intermediate state between waking and dreaming in which certain restrictions and inhibitions imposed by finite reality are lifted. This state may be characterized as romantic in the sense that it is suggestive of the yearning to transcend the barriers of finite reality. The experience of this transmutation of reality, contemplated in retrospect, is reproduced here in a tone of urgency underscored by anaphoric repetition: *"Es entbehrte* der *Einleitung... es*

---

* "Only after the nocturnal vehicle had again set itself into jogging motion did our conversation begin... *It was without introduction,* this conversation, *it was without polite ceremoniousness of any sort; from the very beginning* and *to the very end* it had the *unconditional,* free, and *uncommitted irresponsibility* that is usually characteristic only of dreams, where our ego associates with shadows that have no independent existence, with creations of its own, in a way that is, after all, impossible in waking life where one flesh-and-blood being exists in actual separation from another. Here it happened and I happily admit that I was moved to the *deepest* region of my soul by the *intoxicating strangeness of the experience."*

entbehrte jeder höflichen Umständlichkeit;" by the emphatic crescendo-movement in the adjectival sequence: "die *unbedingte, enthobene* und *entbundene* Unverantwortlichkeit," the components of which amplify the notion of liberation; finally, by the intensifying effect of the superlative "in *tiefster* Seele angesprochen" and the dynamic character of the participial adjective "berauschend".

The immediacy generated by this tone of urgent and penetrating speech is, however, counterbalanced and ultimately impaired by the heavy abstract character of nouns: "Einleitung" ('introduction'), "Umständlichkeit" ('ceremoniousness'), "Unverantwortlichkeit" ('irresponsibility'), "Seltsamkeit" ('strangeness'), and "Vorkommnis" ('happening'). The tendency in such nominality of style is to concentrate the chief denotative stress of each statement in the abstract noun, which has the general effect of lending to the whole the character of rational discourse with its objectives of analysis and definition. The abstraction and rationality form a counterpoint to the tone of urgency with the ultimate effect that whatever romantic or phantastic character may attach to the situation is submerged under the weight of heavy intellectuality and aridity of diction.

This tendency reaches its peak in the proliferation of abstract nouns in the concise summary Krull gives of the substance of his conversation with Rozsa:

> Knapp zusammengefaßt, lief unser Austausch auf die *Bekundung* des lebhaften Gefallens hinaus, das wir sogleich aneinander gefunden, auf die *Erforschung, Erörterung, Zergliederung* dieses Gefallens sowie auf die Abrede, es auf alle Weise zu pflegen, auszubilden und nutzbar zu machen. (380)*

These lines add up to a desiccated and factual report and strike one as having been written by the most pedestrian of mentalities. The style recalls the language of bureaucracy and the legal profession with its tendency to replace verbs with nouns in the interest of conciseness. What is parodistic about these lines is that in relating the affection two people find for each other in a situation enveloped by a suggestive romantic aura a style is employed which is befitting to rational and analytical discourse, but by no means appropriate to the literary or poetic expression of erotic feeling.

Qualification and Contrast

The interpenetration of rational and emotional strains is but one aspect in Thomas Mann's style

---

* "To summarize briefly, our exchange amounted to the *expression* of the lively attraction that we had immediately felt for each other, to the *exploration, discussion,* and *analysis* of this attraction as well as to an agreement to cultivate it in every way, to perfect it, and make it useful."

of a duality which derives from the ironic consciousness and the tendency toward synthesis. As an intellectual attitude, irony may be directed either inward toward the self or outward at the external world and its maze of contradictory and incongruous relationships. Like its prototype, the Socratic dialogue, irony presupposes some form of dialectical tension between opposing forces, "dialogue" and "dialectic" being etymologically related words. In Mann's style an habitual dialectical pattern of thought is reflected in the heavy dependence on disjunctives such as "obgleich," ('although'), "wenn auch" ('even if, though'), and "zwar... aber" ('I admit, to be sure... but'), which have a contrastive and qualifying force and therefore establish dualistic relationships between two or more propositions.[7] The repeated occurrence of these disjunctives is symptomatic of a fundamental duality in the organization of experience, in perception and attitude. In discursive and argumentative writing, of course, the use of disjunctives is not only effective but also natural and inconspicuous, whereas it may be disturbing and even impairing in the expression of intense emotional experience or in lyric poetry. But in Thomas Mann they are of special interest because of their habitual recurrence in character portraits and in the description of states of mind. Indeed, there is hardly a facet of human character and behavior which escapes this aspect of Mann's irony. Its excessive occurrence does not betray an empty mannerism, nor should we view these disjunctives as stylistically neutral elements simply because they are part and parcel of everyday discourse. They yield insights into the author's patterns of thought and experience and uncover his artistic motives.

An element of dualism in the portrayal of both situation and character is already apparent in the opening paragraph of the novel which contains an expository sketch of Krull's family circumstances and of certain outstanding traits of two characters – Godfather Schimmelpreester and Krull's father. As to his family background Krull declares:

> ... ich stamme aus feinbürgerlichem, *wenn auch* liederlichem Hause... (265)*

Introducing first Schimmelpreester and then his father, he relates:

> ... mein Pate Schimmelpreester, mit dem ich auf sehr innigem Fuße stand, war ein vielfach geschätzter Künstler, den jedermann im Städtchen "Herr Professor" nannte, *obgleich* ihm dieser schöne, begehrenswerte Titel von Amts wegen vielleicht nicht einmal zukam; und mein Vater, *wiewohl* dick und fett, besaß viel persönliche Grazie und legte stets Gewicht auf eine

---

* "... I come from an upper-middle-class *though* somewhat dissolute family..."

gewählte und durchsichtige Ausdrucksweise. (265)*

The italicized words are subordinate conjunctions with the force of concession. In addition, they qualify or limit the validity of the previous proposition or, as in the case of "wiewohl", the validity of the proposition that follows. Finally, these disjunctives have the force of bringing two qualities into a relationship of contrast and, ultimately, of ambiguity. As a result, both situation and characters remain suspended in a state of ironic indeterminability. They defy precise classification because of their ambiguity.

Krull's own physical appearance, as we have seen, adds up to this same indeterminateness, which is the outer correlate of his inner character. This indeterminability of outward appearance is heightened to radical intricacy in the portrait of Andromache:

> Ihre Brust war geringfügig, ihr Becken schmal, die Muskulatur ihrer Arme, wie sich versteht, stärker ausgebildet als sonst bei Frauen, und ihre greifenden Hände *zwar nicht* von männ-

* "... My godfather Schimmelpreester, with whom I stood on the most intimate of terms, was a highly esteemed artist whom everyone in our little town called 'Herr Professor,' *though* perhaps officially he was not entitled to this fine and coveted distinction; and my father, *though* corpulent, possessed much personal charm and always laid great stress on the choice and lucid use of words."

licher Größe, *aber doch auch nicht* klein genug, um die Frage ganz auszuschalten, ob sie, in Gottes Namen, denn vielleicht heimlich ein Jüngling sei. *Nein*, die weibliche Artung ihrer Brust war immerhin unzweideutig, und so doch auch, *bei aller* Schlankheit, die Form ihrer Schenkel. (459)*

And a few pages later:

Ein prächtiger Anblick, aber ich gedachte Andromache's. Herrliche Tierleiber, und zwischen Tier und Engel, so sann ich, stehet der Mensch. Näher zum Tiere stehet er, *das wollen wir einräumen*. Sie *aber*, meine Angebetete, *obgleich* Leib ganz und gar, *aber* keuscher, vom Menschlichen ausgeschlossener Leib, stand viel weiter hin zu den Engeln. (461)**

* "Her breasts were meager, her hips narrow, the muscles of her arms, of course, more powerfully developed than is usually the case in women, and her grasping hands, *though* not as big as a man's, were *yet not so small either* as to rule out the question whether she might not, Heaven forbid, be a boy in disguise. *No*, the female conformation of her breasts was unambiguous, and so too, *despite* her slenderness, was the form of her thighs."
** "A splendid sight, but I was thinking of Andromache. Magnificent animal bodies, and it is between animal and angel, so I reflected, that man takes his stand. His place is closer to the animals, *that we must concede*. But she, the one whom I adored, *though* all body – *but* a chaste body, separated from the human – stood much closer to the angels."

THE DIALECTIC OF THE HERMETIC STYLE

In these passages we observe how the question of identity remains unresolved, suspended in a state of indeterminateness, how the decision as to classification pendulates in dialectical tension, is withheld and arrived at only after an involved process of concession, counter-concession, and qualification. It may also be noted in the description of Andromache that the ironic indirectness and indecisiveness of expression is accompanied by an interlarding of the sentence with particles or phrases which have an intensifying force and lend the proposition – despite its complexity of concession, qualification, counter-concession and counter-qualification – an air of positive assertion: "in Gottes Namen" ('Heaven forbid'), "nein" ('no'), "ganz und gar" ('all'), "viel weiter hin" ('*much* closer'). As additional proof of this tendency we may consider the portrait of Isaak Stürzli, the hotel manager:

> Herr Stürzli, ein Mann von ungewöhnlicher Körperfülle... sein Rücken überaus massig gewölbt, sein Nacken äußerst speckig gedrungen... *Dabei* waren seine Hände... erstaunlich klein und zierlich im Verhältnis zu seiner Gesamtmasse, die *aber* überhaupt nichts Unbeholfenes hatte, sondern, wie das zuweilen bei den korpulentesten Leuten vorkommt, eine gewisse elegante Tournure zu bewahren wußte. (410)*

* "Herr Stürzli was a man of unusual corpulence... his back was massively rounded and his neck larded in fatty folds... *By contrast*, his hands... were astonishingly

THE DIALECTIC OF THE HERMETIC STYLE

The initial contrast between the daintiness of hands and a body mass approaching that of a rhinoceros is not minimized but intesified by emphatic words such as "ungewöhnlich," "überaus," "äußerst," and "erstaunlich." But the adverse circumstance of corpulence is quickly offset and brought into balance by a redeeming quality introduced by the contrasting "aber." This positive redeeming quality, however, is arrived at and defined only by way of circumlocution, in the form of an antithesis – "nicht.... sondern"; before we learn what this positive quality *is*, we must first be told quite "definitely" what it *is not*. Contrast expressed by circumlocution – often a litotic expression implying a positive by denying its negative or antithesis – is a pervasive stylistic trait of the work as a whole and is a symptom of irony which thrives on indirectness, mock-objectivity, and ambiguity.[8] As a final example, consider the sketch of Madame Kuckuck which adheres basically to scheme:

> Höher gewachsen als das anziehende Kind, von nicht mehr schlanker, *doch keineswegs* übervoller Gestalt in ihrem einfachen, *aber* vornehmen... Leinenkleid... (561)*

small and delicate in proportion to his over-all mass about which, *however*, there was nothing at all awkward; *on the contrary*, as is sometimes the case in corpulent people, he maintained a certain elegance of movement."
* "Taller than her attractive child, no longer slender *but by no means* too full... in her simple *but* distinguished linen dress..."

A slightly adverse trait is suggested by means of a litotic expression: "nicht mehr schlank"; this is followed by a contrasting "doch" which, together with the intensifier "keineswegs" – a negative particle with the force of positive and emphatic assertion – immediately seeks to eliminate the possibility of an erroneous impression.[9] This exaggerated desire to be just and accurate in the description of character is not to be equated with mere pedantic fastidiousness. The unique combination of indirectness and precision, of ironic treatment and sympathetic involvement, is an expression of the duality of an ironic consciousness. In Mann's dialectical sentence-structure intensification and crescendo, while reverberating as the rhythmical and emotional background, stand in contrapuntal relationship to the cool objectivity and rationality of diction of the main discursive line.

The Oxymoron

The heightened and, at the same time, more subtle manifestation of the duality of Mann's style is the syntactical linking of contaries or the *oxymoron*. The particular form of the oxymoron may vary from the fusion of two contraries in a compound adjective ("bittersweet"), the collocation of adjective and noun – which is often called *contradictio in adjecto* and constitutes the most frequently occurring type in *Felix Krull* – to the contradictory relationship involved in the combination of adverb and verb or of adverb and adjective. The oxymoron may, however, in a more general sense apply to any statement with two seemingly contradictory components. Defined thus, the syntactical combination of contraries connected by "and" may also be called an oxymoron.

In our first example the reference is to Krull's visits to Godfather Schimmelpreester's atelier where he posed nude for a tableau depicting a mythological motif. As we noted earlier, this circumstance occasions a narcissistic description of Krull's physique:

> Hierbei erntete ich viel Lob von seiten des Künstlers, denn ich war überaus angenehm und göttergleich gewachsen, schlank, *weich und doch kräftig* von Gliedern, goldig von Haut und ohne Tadel in Hinsicht auf schönes Ebenmaß. (284)*

Of special interest is the phrase "weich und doch kräftig" ('delicate and yet powerful') which has in common with some of the previously cited examples the use of "doch" with its contrasting and qualifying force. Yet it differs from the other examples in that the semantic relationship between the two qualities suggests a contradiction. Contrast is here heightened to the level of paradox.

---

* "I gained much praise from the artist, for my stature was extremely pleasing and godlike, slender, *delicate and yet powerful* in build, golden in skin, and flawless with respect to symmetry of proportion."

Striking as the combination is, however, the careful reader will, on reflection, discover a hidden compatibility. Taken in their literal and denotative meaning, the qualities "weich" and "kräftig" strike us as contradictory. But if "weich" is understood in its figurative sense of "supple in form," the combination becomes more conceivable. The underlying stylistic technique is that of linking two qualities, the relationship of which strikes us initially as contradictory if we associate the words with their literal and everyday meanings. It is the reader's habits of association that are exploited. The paradoxical formulation causes the attentive reader to re-examine, to reflect, to reevaluate, to work out the synthesis for himself. The contradiction in such a combination is more accurately described as a psychological, rather than a logical, contradiction.

The syntactical pattern of "weich und doch kräftig" is also important. It is noteworthy that in such a formulation the qualities appear contrasted rather than fused, coexistent rather than coalescent. It is the "doch" that is instrumental in suggesting this contrasting force. The "und" graphically links, but does not fuse. To make this point clearer, let us consider a slightly modified recurrence of essentially the same idea but in a different syntactical pattern in the later part of the work. The effect is one of *leitmotif* when, in the boudoir scene, Diane Philibert extolls the physical attractiveness of Krull's body in the following words:

THE DIALECTIC OF THE HERMETIC STYLE

> ... hilf Himmel, bist du schön! Die Brust so süß in ihrer *weichen und klaren Strenge*, der schlanke Arm, die holden Rippen, eingezogenen Hüften, und ach, die Hermes-Beine... (444)*

Here the quality of "weich" is not contrasted or qualified by means of "doch" or "aber", but coalesces with the abstract noun "Strenge." Mann stylistically fuses these contrary qualities into synthesis. The addition of a third quality – "klar" – mitigates the dualistic tension between "weich" and "Strenge" so that the sum total of the qualities in combination approaches the subtle nuance. Taken as a whole, the contrast is less obtrusive not only by the absence of a contrasting "doch," but also because the contraries occur here in attributive rather than in predicate position. The predicate adjective, owing to its post-position in a sentence and to the absence – in German – of inflected endings, generally tends to receive heavier stress and is thus brought into greater prominence; the attributive adjective, by contrast, with its inflected ending in combination with a noun, has a less obtrusive, more casual effect.[10] The combination, to be sure, is still striking, the semantic relationship between the components still conflicting, but the tendency – reflected in the stylistic

---

* "... heaven help me, how beautiful you are! The breast so sweet in its *smooth and clear severity*, the slender arms, the noble ribs, the narrow hips, and, oh, the Hermes legs..."

pattern – is toward subtle nuance and fusion of contraries into a synthesis. The deeper significance of this fusion is that it reflects Krull's androgyny. The dualistic combination of "weich" and "kräftig" or "weich" and "streng" fused in synthesis is the symbolic union of feminine grace and masculine vigor.

The artistic intention in the use of the oxymoron will, of course, vary depending on the object or circumstance to which it applies. Ironic debunking appears to be the motive in the following passage which contains a distinct oxymoron:

> Mit kurzem Kopfnicken (denn der Cirkus kennt nicht die Verbeugung) quittiert der Artist den rauschenden Beifall der die Runde füllenden Menge, dieses einzigartigen Publikums, das sich aus gierigem Schaupöbel und einer Pferde-Lebewelt von *roher Eleganz* erregend und beklemmend zusammensetzt. (456)*

The habitual pattern of Thomas Mann's thought and experience, namely, to perceive and record phenomena in pairs, either in the form of duality or of contrast, pervades this passage from beginning to end. First, there is the parenthetical aside

---

* "With a brief nod (for the circus does not use the bow) the artist acknowledges the ecstatic applause of the massed onlookers, this unique audience, excitingly and oppressingly composed of the sensation-seeking masses and the *rude elegance* of the horsy playboy set."

which contrasts the typical or general with the unique. Secondly, the audience is composed of two segments – "the sensation-seeking masses" and "the horsy playboy set," the latter of which, however, is not altogether too distinct from the former owing to the ironic pairing of "roh" – a quality which it has in common with the former – with "Eleganz." Finally, there is the dual adverbial expression "erregend und beklemmend," the components of which do not contradict, but supplement each other and fuse into a nuance. Another effect of the oxymoron here is suggested by the reference to the audience as "unique": the striking and unconventional oxymoron is one of the most effective stylistic devices for lending characters, situations, and complex states of mind the utmost of originality and individuality.

This habitual pattern of thought and perception, as it manifests itself in Thomas Mann's style, has its intellectual correlate in a dominant motif-complex in the novel – the fascination with the "double-but-dissimilar," and the longing for unity, paradoxically, in duality. Only in the double, in a combination of complementary aspects, does Krull perceive both beauty and a significant whole. The fact that this motif is sounded for the first time in Mann's revised episode of the brother-sister pair on the balcony – the joint between the earlier fragment and the later part of the novel –[11] coincides with the prevalent stylistic tendency of the later part toward syntactical fusion of contrary or disparate elements into a whole compared to their manifestation in the early fragment where the relationship is one of contrast or coexistence.

Altogether these examples of stylistic traits demonstrate with obtrusive clarity that Thomas Mann is a highly conscious stylist. These features, however, are not peculiar to the *Confessions of Felix Krull*, but are in evidence as trademarks of Mann's fictional craft in virtually all his major works. They constitute the linguistic counterpart and fulfillment of the aesthetic concern symbolized in the emblem of the arrow and the lyre: the unification of opposites. But in *Felix Krull* Mann has created with consummate artistic skill a unity between style and theme which is particularly impressive because of its polyvalency. Mann's dialectical sentence structure and his oxymora correspond on the thematic level to the ambiguous identity of the hero, the ambivalence in his attitude toward the world, the duality of his perception, his Hermes-Mercurius capacity of mediating between and also uniting within himself all conceivable opposites, and to the dialectic interplay of opposing psychological forces in Krull's development toward a synthesis of ego-libido and object-libido, of a highly cultivated ego-consciousness and the transpersonal nature of the unconscious.

Of Thomas Mann's fictional heroes, only Felix Krull is unmistakably and far-reachingly identifiable with Hermes. The genesis of this last of Mann's novels to be published and the development of its protagonist's consciousness exhibit, finally, a significant correlation with the history of Mann's own consciousness. Just as Felix Krull's awareness of his identity with Hermes is a relatively late occurrence in the plot of the work – though his early character is a preconscious prefiguration of it – so also was Mann's awareness of the identity between his artistic concern of union of opposites and Hermes-Mercurius as mediator and unifier par excellence a late development. Mann's confession to Kerenyi that of all mythological gods Hermes was the one with whom he was becoming ever more preoccupied is the testimony of a richly associative mind which found encompassed within a single archetypal symbol the admirable representation of his own fundamental artistic concerns in both theme and style.

The symbolical wedlock of myth and psychoanalysis – another favorite and early association of Thomas Mann – became an actuality in the scholarly collaboration of Kerenyi and Jung. One of the fruits of this marriage was the density of mythic and psychological associations skillfully woven into the colorful tapestry of *Felix Krull*.

NOTES: I. INTRODUCTION

[1] For a treatment of the connections between *Felix Krull* and the Picaresque novel see Oskar Seidlin, "Picaresque Elements in Thomas Mann's Work," *Modern Language Quarterly*, 12, No. 2 (1951), 183-200. Also Robert B. Heilman, "Variations on Picaresque," *Sewanee Review*, 66 (1958), 547-577.

[2] This is the view of Eva Schiffer, "Illusion und Wirklichkeit in Thomas Manns 'Felix Krull' und 'Joseph,'" *Monatshefte für deutschen Unterricht*, 55 (1963), 70.

[3] The most detailed studies on the Hermes-motif in Thomas Mann's work are Walter Jens, *Statt einer Literaturgeschichte* (Pfullingen; Neske, 1957), pp. 89-107; the unpublished dissertation of Jürgen Plöger, "Das Hermesmotiv in der Dichtung Thomas Manns," Kiel 1960; Helmut Koopmann, *Die Entwicklung des intellektualen Romans bei Thomas Mann*, (Bonn: Bouvier, 1962), pp. 155-168. A typical generalization that is indisputable but begs elaboration is Koopmann's statement: "Krull selbst *ist* auch Hermes – der Besuch bei Madame Houpflé hat mythische Hintergründe: er wird zum Spiel zwischen Hermes, dem geschmeidigen Gott der Diebe, und Diana. Immer wird das Mythische in spaßhaft grotesker Form behandelt; der Mythus wird ständig ironisiert, zuweilen sogar parodiert, aber doch so, daß das mythische Substrat als solches stets erkennbar bleibt" (p. 154). However, Koopmann is really most concerned with the motif in "Der Zauberberg." Here, his analysis advances our understanding much more. He analyzes what he calls "Die Kategorie des Hermetischen" in both characters and the spatial and temporal structures of the novel. Jürgen Plöger traces the motif at length in the Joseph cycle, but devotes relatively few pages to *Felix Krull*. His study is the most detailed to date, but remains at the level of listing and description. The statements of Walter Jens are so general that at times it is difficult to determine whether the epithets he cites ("der Vermittler, der Schalk, der Seelengeleiter,

der Lebensspender und Todesbote, der Listige und Geistvolle, Erotisch-Wendige und Beharrlich-Schlaue") apply to Joseph or to Krull or to both. The sum of his reasoning, as I have been able to gather it, is the following: "In Tadzio, Joseph und Felix verkörpert Hermes die Vollkommenheit der menschlichen Figur, die Form an sich, gepaart mit Anmut und Geist" (p. 106).

[4] Frederick J. Hoffman, *Freudianism and the Literary Mind* (Baton Rouge: Louisiana State University Press, 1945), sees the aesthetic development of the Joseph stories indebted to Freud's theories of the racial unconscious. In many respects his treatment is a restatement and elaboration of Mann's own ideas in the essay "Freud and the Future." Hoffman stresses Mann's acceptance of psychoanalysis as a "protection against irrational forces" (p. 209). He points out the connections between Freud's analysis of the unconscious as an essentially timeless entity and Mann's emphasis on the suspension of historical time, recurrence, and the continuity of racial memory as basic elements of myth. By contrast, Adèle Bloch, "The Archetypal Influences in Thomas Mann's 'Joseph and His Brothers,'" *Germanic Review*, 38 (1963), 151-156, argues that in the Joseph cycle "Mann adheres to the Jungian theory of archetypes while showing that personal life reproduces that of the entire human race." This argument is supported by references to "Freud and the Future" in which Mann gives credit to Jung for having formulated the anima projection theory by which the God image born from within is externalized, an idea which figures significantly in the characterization of Joseph. In brief outline, dominant motifs of the Joseph cycle are related to such Jungian archetypal motifs as androgyny, separation from the mother, projection of the anima image, the ambivalence of the Great Mother, and the synthesis of Ego and Unconscious through the perilous descent. The only regrettable aspect of this fine essay is that its brevity

does not permit elaboration of these ideas.

[5] In *Totem and Taboo*, trans. James Strachey (New York: Norton and Co., 1962), p. 157, Freud states: "... I have taken as the basis of my whole position the existence of a collective mind, in which mental processes occur just as they do in the mind of an individual."

[6] For an historical account of the movement see R. H. Lowie, *The History of Ethnological Theory* (New York: Farrar and Rinehart, 1937).

[7] Franz Alexander, *The Western Mind in Transition* (New York: Random House, 1960), p. 193, expresses a psychoanalytic position: "The instinctual drives, the aspirations and the conflicts of western man today appear not much different from what we can reconstruct from Greek, Roman or medieval literature. In all ages, people loved and hated, competed and cooperated, sought security and adventure, hoped and despaired, adjusted themselves to conditions and created new environments to live in. While these basic components of human nature remained unchanged, attitudes toward the universe, social behavior and values show well-defined, if not consistent, variations." In *Our Age of Unreason*, rev. ed. (New York: Lippincott, 1951), p. 7, Alexander states the relationship between basic unchanging psychological structure and cultural differences thus: "In the deep unconscious all men are akin; individuality is formed nearer the surface. Ego-psychology permits us to recognize and estimate those features of personality which are molded by the cultural environment and are superimposed upon a more or less uniform biological and emotional substratum." For a summary of the trend in recent cultural anthropology toward defining cultural universals and the influence of psychoanalysis upon anthropology see Paul Roazen, *Freud: Political and Social Thought* (New York: Knopf, 1968), pp. 36-75.

[8] *Imago*, 21 (1935), 320-344.

[9] I am indebted for this suggestion to Joseph Campbell,

"Bios and Mythos: Prolegomena to a Science of Mythology," in *Myth and Literature*, ed. John B. Vickery (Lincoln: Univ. of Nebraska Press, 1966), p. 16.

[10] This view is persuasively argued and demonstrated by Joseph L. Blotner, "Mythic Patterns in 'To the Lighthouse,'" in *Myth and Literature*, ed. John B. Vickery, pp. 243-255.

[11] The most informative letter in this respect is that of Mann to Kerenyi, dated Feb. 18, 1941. In this letter Mann acknowledges receipt of Kerenyi's *Das göttliche Kind* which was first published as volumes 6 and 7 of the series Albae Vigiliae (Zürich: Rhein Verlag, 1941). It was subsequently incorporated into the joint work of Jung and Kerenyi, *Einführung in das Wesen der Mythologie* (Zürich: Rhein-Verlag, 1951). The following extracts clearly reveal Mann's familiarity with Jungian interpretations of myth: "... daß Sie sich wissenschaftlich mit Jung zusammenfanden, die Mythologie mit der Psychologie, ist ein sehr merkwürdiges, erfreuliches und für den geistigen Augenblick hochcharakteristisches Ereignis. Das 'Göttliche Kind' hat mich richtig erreicht. Es ist ein extrem-interessantes Buch – kein Wunder, daß es ein Wunder an Interessantheit gibt, wenn zwei Eingeweihte von diesen Graden sich zusammentun. Es würde Sie amüsieren, zu sehen, mit wieviel An- und Unterstreichungen die Seiten meines Exemplares bedeckt sind. Für mein Teil habe ich mich gefreut, zu sehen, wie eifrig und aufgeregt ich noch lesen kann, wenn ich wirklich in meinem Elemente bin, – und was sollte mein Element derzeit wohl sein als Mythos plus Psychologie. Längst bin ich ein leidenschaftlicher Freund dieser Combination... Sie sehen, was Ihr Gemeinschaftswerk mir schon prinzipiell alles bedeutet... Den Psychopompos als wesentlich kindliche Gottheit gekennzeichnet zu sehen, mußte mich freuen: es erinnerte mich an Tadzio im 'Tod in Venedig'. Und den hermetischen Mangel an 'Einheit der Person', von dem Jung spricht,

NOTES: I

habe ich in den 'Geschichten Jaakobs' ganz auf eigene Hand als humoristische Tatsache behandelt... Die mythologische Figur, die mich jetzt notwendiger Weise mehr und mehr anzieht, und über die ich wieder soviel Schönes in diesem Buche fand, ist der mondverbundene Hermes. Er spukte schon bisher da und dort durch die Joseph-Bücher; aber im letzten Bande, der den Helden als Staats-Geschäftsmann von reichlicher Durchtriebenheit zeigt, wechselt dieser aus der ursprünglichen Tammuz-Adonis-Rolle immer mehr in die eines Hermes hinüber. Seine Aktionen und Transaktionen sind moralisch-ästhetisch nicht gut anders zu vertreten, als im Sinne des göttlichen Schelmen-Romans" (Karl Kerenyi, *Romandichtung und Mythologie*, Zürich: Rhein-Verlag, 1945, pp. 82-83). ("... that you have come together with Jung, mythology with psychology, is a very noteworthy and delightful event. I have received your book, 'Das Göttliche Kind.' It is an extremely interesting book – no wonder that there are wonderfully interesting things when two adepts of such stature get together. You would be amused to see how many pencil markings there are on the pages of my copy. I have been pleased to note how I can still read with zeal and excitement when I am really in my element – and what should my element be at present other than myth plus psychology. I have been an ardent enthusiast of this combination for a long time... You can see how important your joint project has been for me... I could not fail to be delighted at seeing the *psychopompos* characterized as an essentially childlike deity: it reminded me of Tadzio in *Death in Venice*. And the hermetic lack of 'unity of person,' of which Jung speaks, is something which I treated in my own way as a humorous fact in *The Tales of Jacob*... The mythological figure who at present is attracting me more and more and about whom I found so many beautiful things in this book is Hermes who is closely bound up with the moon. His spectral presence may be found now and then in the early Joseph-stories; but in the last volume, which depicts the hero as a statesman and businessman of considerable shrewdness, the protagonist passes more and more from his original role of Tammuz-Adonis into that of Hermes. His actions and transactions can hardly be represented better, morally and aesthetically, than in the sense of a divine Picaresque novel"). Mann's enthusiasm in the above quoted letter stands in curious contrast to a note of cool reserve in the following letter of Feb. 22, 1945 to Anna Jacobson which appears to be a response to an inquiry concerning the influence of Jung on Mann: "Jung habe ich in der Schweiz nie gesehen. Er besuchte mich einmal in München zusammen mit einem anderen Herrn, an den ich mich nicht mehr erinnere. Jung machte einen außerordentlich gescheiten Eindruck auf mich. Seine Haltung gegenüber den Nazis war anfangs recht zweifelhaft und mehr als das. Literarische Beziehungen haben nie bestanden" (Thomas Mann, *Briefe* 1937-1947 [Frankfurt: Fischer, 1963], p. 413). ("I never saw Jung in Switzerland. He visited me once in Munich together with another gentlemen whom I don't remember any more. Jung impressed me as being an exceptionally intelligent person. His position toward the Nazis was in the beginning more than dubious. Literary connections have never existed").

[12] In a letter of March 24, 1934 to Kerenyi (*Romandichtung*), Mann notes that he has received a copy of Walter F. Otto's *Die Götter Griechenlands* and that he is about to begin reading it. Kerenyi had previously recommended this book to him: "Wer und was alles Hermes ist, schildert unübertrefflich Walter F. Otto in seinem Buch 'Die Götter Griechenlands' (Bonn 1929), das Sie – wenn Sie mir diese dringliche Empfehlung verzeihen – unbedingt lesen müßten" (*Romandichtung*, p. 23).

NOTES: II. BEYOND GOOD AND EVIL

[1] J. G. Frazer, *The Magic Art*, I (London: Macmillan, 1911), 240.
[2] Norman O. Brown, *Hermes the Thief* (Madison: Univ. of Wisconsin Press, 1947), p. 19.
[3] Brown, p. 11.
[4] Brown, pp. 9-10, 21-22.
[5] Brown, p. 9.
[6] Brown, p. 22.
[7] Walter F. Otto, *The Homeric Gods*, trans. Moses Hadas (New York: Pantheon, 1954), p. 115.
[8] Otto, p. 117.
[9] Otto, p. 105.
[10] Otto, pp. 122-123.
[11] Plöger, "Das Hermesmotiv," 160, argues that any suggestion of the Hermes-motif in the earlier (i.e., pre-1937) version of *Felix Krull* is "minimal" and does not warrant the conclusion that Hermes figured in Mann's original conception. Strictly speaking, these two propositions are not mutually exclusive. However minimal evidence may be, it still exists as evidence.

NOTES: III. HERMAPHRODITUS AND THE PRIMAL HERMES

[1] For an orientation to the problem see Marie Delcourt, *Hermaphrodite*, trans. Jennifer Nicholson (London: Studio Books, 1961), pp. 46-66.
[2] In a letter to Kerenyi, dated Dec. 3, 1945, Mann warmly acknowledges receipt of a number of books and articles among which was *Hermes der Seelenführer*. See *Briefe* 1937-1947 (Frankfurt: Fischer, 1963), p. 460 and p. 706.
[3] Karl Kerenyi, *Hermes der Seelenführer* (Zürich: Rhein-Verlag, 1944), pp. 73-77. See also C. G. Jung and C. Kerenyi, *Essays on a Science of Mythology*, trans. R. F. C. Hull (New York: Pantheon, 1949), p. 74.
[4] *Hermes der Seelenführer*, p. 74.
[5] In medieval alchemy Hermes and Mercury are represented as hermaphroditic. This subject will be treated in Chapter 7 of this book.
[6] *Hermes der Seelenführer*, pp. 73-77.
[7] Cicero, *De natura deorum*, ed. Joseph B. Mayor (Cambridge, Eng.: University Press, 1885), III 22, 60.
[8] *De natura deorum*, III 22, 56-59.
[9] *Sexti Propertii Elegiarum*, ed. Petrus Johannes Enk (Leyden: A. W. Sythoff, 1962), II 2, 11.
[10] *Hermes der Seelenführer*, p. 75. For a more detailed discussion of this complex relationship see also Jung and Kerenyi, *Essays*, pp. 154-158.

NOTES: IV. DIVINE ANDROGYNY AND SELF-SUFFICIENT NARCISSISM

[1] I am very much indebted for this insight to Marie Delcourt, *Hermaphrodite*, pp. 56-66.
[2] Mircea Eliade, *Patterns in Comparative Religion*, trans. Rosemary Sheed (London: Sheed and Ward, 1958), pp. 420-423.
[3] C. G. Jung, *Mysterium Coniunctionis*, trans. R. F. C. Hull, Vol. XIV of *The Collected Works* (New York: Pantheon, 1963), p. 374 – hereafter cited as *Works*.
[4] *Aion*, Vol. IX, Part 2 of *Works*, 2nd ed. (Princeton: Princeton Univ. Press, 1968), p. 204.
[5] *Aion*, p. 205.
[6] For an extensive treatment of this subject see Mircea Eliade, *The Two and the One*, trans. J. M. Cohen (London: Harvill Press, 1965), pp. 78-124.
[7] Jung, *Alchemical Studies*, Vol. XIII of *Works* (Princeton: Princeton Univ. Press, 1967), p. 217.
[8] My statements on narcissism are based on Freud's article, "On Narcissism: An Introduction," in Vol. XIV of the *Standard Edition of the Complete Psychological Works of Sigmund Freud*, trans. James Strachey (London: Hogarth Press, 1957), pp. 73-102.
[9] *Symbols of Transformation*, Vol. V of *Works* (New York: Pantheon, 1956), p. 173.
[10] "On Narcissism," p. 82.
[11] "On Narcissism," p. 98.
[12] "On Narcissism," pp. 99-100.

NOTES: V. DIANA THE PROVIDER

[1] *The Homeric Gods*, p. 88.
[2] "Die Kunst der Epik ist 'apollinische' Kunst... denn Apollo, der Fernhintreffende, ist der Gott der Ferne, der Gott der Distanz, der Objektivität, der Gott der Ironie. Objektivität ist Ironie, und der epische Kunstgeist ist der Geist der Ironie." (X, 353)
[3] *The Golden Bough*, Vol. I, abridged ed. (New York: Macmillan, 1922), pp. 141-142.
[4] Jung, *Two Essays on Analytical Psychology*, Vol. VII of *Works* (New York: Pantheon, 1953), p. 190.
[5] On the identity of Artemis, Persephone, and Hecate see Jung-Kerenyi, *Essays on a Science of Mythology*, pp. 148-158.
[6] Karl Kerenyi, *Apollon. Studien über antike Religion und Humanität*, 2nd rev. ed. (Amsterdam: Akademische Verlagsanstalt Pantheon, 1941), p. 157.
[7] For this connection I am indebted to W. F. Otto, *The Homeric Gods*, p. 108.
[8] Thomas Bulfinch, *The Age of Fable* (London: J. M. Dent, and New York: E. P. Dutton, 1960), p. 207.

NOTES: VI. THE ELEUSINIAN MYSTERIES REVISITED

1. *Hermaphrodite*, p. 43.
2. *Romandichtung und Mythologie*, pp. 77-78.
3. Karl Kerenyi, *Eleusis. Archetypal Image of Mother and Daughter*, trans. Ralph Manheim (New York: Pantheon, 1967), pp. 32-33. Also: Erich Neumann, *The Great Mother*, trans. Ralph Manheim (New York: Pantheon, 1955), pp. 305-325.
4. Neumann, *The Great Mother*, p. 307.
5. Ibid.
6. Kerenyi, *Eleusis*, p. 33.
7. Jung, *The Archetypes and the Collective Unconscious*, Vol. IX, Part 1, 2nd ed. of *Works* (Princeton: Princeton Univ. Press, 1968), p. 81.
8. Ibid.
9. *Aion*, pp. 11-22.
10. *The Great Mother*, p. 8.
11. Ibid., p. 75.
12. *The Great Mother*, p. 34.
13. *The Archetypes and the Collective Unconscious*, p. 185.
14. Erich Neumann, *The Origins and History of Consciousness*, trans. R. F. C. Hull (New York: Pantheon, 1954), p. 155.
15. Neuman, *The Great Mother*, pp. 317-325. See also: Jung, *The Archetypes*, p. 203.
16. *The Great Mother*, p. 43.
17. *The Great Mother*, p. 306.
18. *The Great Mother*, pp. 189-190.
19. Jung, *Symbols of Transformation*, p. 435.
20. For a comparison between the symbolical meaning of the Mithraic and the Christian sacrifice see Jung, *Symbols of Transformation*, pp. 433-434.
21. *The Great Mother*, pp. 190-208.
22. *The Great Mother*, p. 192.
23. Jung-Kerenyi, *Essays*, p. 171.
24. Neumann, *The Origins and History of Consciousness*, p. 162.
25. Ibid., p. 163.
26. Jung-Kerenyi, *Essays*, p. 134.

NOTES: VII. MERCURIUS, ALCHEMY, AND THE UNION OF OPPOSITES

[1] *Mysterium Coniunctionis*, pp. 457-553.
[2] Ibid., p. 462.
[3] Ibid.
[4] Ibid.
[5] Ibid., p. 463.
[6] Jung, *Psychology and Alchemy*, Vol. XII, 2nd ed. of *Works* (Princeton: Princeton Univ. Press, 1968), p. 372.
[7] Jung, *Alchemical Studies*, p. 207.
[8] *Psychology and Alchemy*, p. 66.
[9] *Alchemical Studies*, p. 217.
[10] *Psychology and Alchemy*, p. 293.
[11] Ibid., p. 292.

NOTES: VIII. THE DIALECTIC OF THE HERMETIC STYLE

[1] *The Homeric Gods*, p. 76.
[2] Oskar Seidlin, "Der junge Joseph und der alte Fontane," in *Festschrift für Richard Alewyn*, ed. Herbert Singer and Benno von Wiese (Köln: Böhlau Verlag, 1967), pp. 384-391, interprets Mann's choice of the arrow and the lyre for his emblem as a borrowing from Fontane's novel *Effi Briest* in which Alonzo Gieshübler seals a letter to his adored Effi with a wafer bearing the sign of a lyre and an arrow. My statement above is not intended as a refutation of Seidlin's interpretation – which I consider persuasive – but only as a suggestion that Mann may have taken delight in the later discovery that the range of association attaching to his emblem also included the idea of synthesis. Since the provenience of Mann's symbol is one thing and its meaning another, it is still possible that Mann may have originally associated some idea of synthesis with the emblem. While it is true that Otto speaks only of the bow and the lyre and not the arrow and the lyre, Mann's early statement in "Bilse und Ich" (cf. p. 108 above) also makes explicit reference only to "the strict bow" and "the sweet lyre." The epithets "streng" and "süß" suggest contraries.
[3] X, 863.
[4] IX, 29.
[5] X, 420.
[6] Here and henceforth all italics in quoted passages are mine.
[7] Detailed and systematic analyses of the function and semantic force of conjunctions and adverbs may be found in the following works, all of which are in fundamental agreement with one another: George O. Curme, *A Grammar of the German Language* (London: Macmillan, 1905); Wilhelm Schneider, *Stilistische deutsche Grammatik* (Freiburg: Herder, 1959); Hennig Brinkmann, *Die deutsche Sprache* (Düsseldorf: Schwann, 1962).
[8] The frequencies of these phenomena are as follows: the *litotes* occurs 80 times in the work as a whole or an

average of once every five pages; the antithetical *nicht ... sondern* pattern ('not... but') occurs 106 times or an average of once every four pages.

[9] Wilhelm Schneider, *Stilistische deutsche Grammatik*, pp. 281-285, classifies such adverbs as "durchaus" ('by all means'), "schlechterdings" ('utterly'), "ganz und gar" ('totally'), "sicherlich" ('surely'), "stets" ('always'), "immer" ('always') together with "keineswegs" and "keinesfalls" ('by no means') as adverbs that lend a style the character of definitive and positive assertion.

[10] This is persuasively demonstrated on the basis of contrastive examples by Schneider, *Stilistische deutsche Grammatik*, pp. 63-64.

[11] To my knowledge, Eva Schiffer, "Changes in an Episode. A Note on Felix Krull," *Modern Language Quarterly*, 24 (1963), 257-262, is the first to point out that this revised episode has both a decisive structural and thematic significance for the work in that it shows "Mann's deliberate use of the revised chapter as a link between the earlier and final versions of the novel" besides clarifying and stressing what is a central theme in the work as a whole.

SELECTED BIBLIOGRAPHY

Alexander, Franz. *Our Age of Unreason.* Rev. ed. New York: Lippincott, 1951.
— *The Western Mind in Transition.* New York: Random House, 1960.
Bloch, Adèle. "The Archetypal Influences in Thomas Mann's 'Joseph and His Brothers,'" *Germanic Review,* 38 (1963), 151-156.
Brinkmann, Hennig. *Die deutsche Sprache.* Düsseldorf: Schwann, 1962.
Brown, Norman O. *Hermes the Thief.* Madison: Univ. of Wisconsin Press, 1947.
Bulfinch, Thomas. *The Age of Fable.* London: J. M. Dent, and New York: E. P. Dutton, 1960.
Cicero, Marcus Tullius. *De natura deorum,* ed. Joseph B. Mayor. Cambridge, Eng.: University Press, 1885.
Curme, George O. *A Grammar of the German Language.* London: Macmillan, 1905.
Delcourt, Marie. *Hermaphrodite,* trans. Jennifer Nicholson. London: Studio Books, 1961.
Eliade, Mircea. *Patterns in Comparative Religion,* trans. Rosemary Sheed. London: Sheed and Ward, 1958.
— *The Two and the One,* trans. J. M. Cohen. London: Harvill Press, 1965.
Frazer, Sir James George. *The Magic Art and the Evolution of Kings.* 3rd ed. London: Macmillan, 1911.
— *The Golden Bough.* Abridged ed. New York: Macmillan, 1922.
Freud, Sigmund. "On Narcissism," *Standard Edition of the Complete Psychological Works of Sigmund Freud,* trans. James Strachey, vol. XIV, pp. 73-102. London: Hogarth Press, 1957.
Hoffman, Frederick J. *Freudianism and the Literary Mind.* Baton Rouge: Louisiana State Univ. Press, 1945.
Jens, Walter. *Statt einer Literaturgeschichte.* Pfullingen: Neske, 1957.
Jung, Carl G. *Symbols of Transformation,* trans. R. F. C. Hull, vol. V of *Collected Works.* New York: Pantheon, 1956.

— *Two Essays on Analytical Psychology*, trans. R. F. C. Hull, vol. VII of *Collected Works*. New York: Pantheon, 1953.
— *The Archetypes and the Collective Unconscious*, trans. R. F. C. Hull, vol. IX, part 1, 2nd ed. of *Collected Works*. Princeton: Princeton Univ. Press, 1968.
— *Aion*, trans. R. F. C. Hull, vol. IX, part 2, 2nd ed. of *Collected Works*. Princeton: Princeton Univ. Press, 1968.
— *Psychology and Alchemy*, trans. R. F. C. Hull, vol. XII of *Collected Works*. Princeton: Princeton Univ. Press, 1968.
— *Alchemical Studies*, trans. R. F. C. Hull, vol. XIII of *Collected Works*. Princeton: Princeton Univ. Press, 1967.
— *Mysterium Coniunctionis*, trans. R. F. C. Hull, vol. XIV of *Collected Works*. New York: Pantheon, 1963.
Jung, Carl G. and Carl Kerenyi. *Essays on a Science of Mythology: The Myth of the Divine Child and the Mysteries of Eleusis*, trans. R. F. C. Hull. New York: Pantheon, 1949.
Kerenyi, Karl. *Apollon. Studien über antike Religion und Humanität*. 2nd rev. ed. Amsterdam: Akademische Verlagsanstalt Pantheon, 1941.
— *Hermes der Seelenführer*. Zürich: Rhein-Verlag, 1944.
— *Romandichtung und Mythologie: Ein Briefwechsel mit Thomas Mann*. Zürich: Rhein-Verlag, 1945.
— *Eleusis: Archetypal Image of Mother and Daughter*, trans. Ralph Manheim. New York: Pantheon, 1967.
Koopmann, Helmut. *Die Entwicklung des intellektualen Romans bei Thomas Mann*. Bonn: Bouvier, 1962.
Kris, Ernst, "Zur Psychologie älterer Biographik," *Imago*, 21 (1935).
Lowie, Robert H. *The History of Ethnological Theory*. New York: Farrar and Rinehart, 1937.
Mann, Thomas. *Gesammelte Werke in Zwölf Bänden*. Frankfurt: Fischer, 1960.

SELECTED BIBLIOGRAPHY

— *Briefe* 1937-1947. Frankfurt: Fischer, 1963.
Myth and Literature. Ed. John B. Vickery. Lincoln: Univ. of Nebraska Press, 1966.
Neumann, Erich. *The Origins and History of Consciousness*, trans. R. F. C. Hull. New York: Pantheon, 1954.
— *The Great Mother*, trans. Ralph Manheim. New York: Pantheon, 1955.
Otto, Walter F. *The Homeric Gods*, trans. Moses Hadas. New York: Pantheon, 1954.
Plöger, Jürgen. "Das Hermesmotiv in der Dichtung Thomas Manns." Unpubl. diss. Kiel, 1960.
Roazen, Paul. *Freud: Political and Social Thought.* New York: Knopf, 1968.
Schiffer, Eva. "Illusion und Wirklichkeit in Thomas Manns 'Felix Krull' und 'Joseph,'" *Monatshefte für deutschen Unterricht*, 55 (1963), 70.
— "Changes in an Episode: A Note on Felix Krull," *Modern Language Quarterly*, 24 (1963), 257-262.
Schneider, Wilhelm. *Stilistische deutsche Grammatik.* Freiburg: Herder, 1959.
Seidlin, Oskar. "Picaresque Elements in Thomas Mann's Work," *Modern Language Quarterly*, 12, No. 2 (1951), 183-200.
— "Der junge Joseph und der alte Fontane." *Festschrift für Richard Alewyn.* Ed. Herbert Singer und Benno von Wiese. Köln: Böhlau Verlag, 1967, pp. 384-391.
Wysling, Hans and Paul Scherrer. *Quellenkritische Studien zum Werk Thomas Manns.* Bern and München: Francke, 1967.
Wysling, Hans. *Mythos und Psychologie bei Thomas Mann.* Zürich: Polygraphischer Verlag, 1969.

GENERAL INDEX

above and below, interchangeability of, 83
abstract noun, effect of in Mann's style, 112-113
Adam
    as originally bisexual, 32
    as prototype of androgyny, 68
Adonis, 32
Alcaeus, 18
Alcithoe, 21
Alexander, Franz
    Our Age of Unreason, 131
    The Western Mind in Transition, 131
altruism, 65
ambivalence
    and divinities, 12, 33, 46, 63, 80
    and Krull's character, 15-16, 33-37, 97, 126
    see also mother archetype
analogy
    as underlying principle in mythopoeic criticism, 7-8
    distinguished from homology, 6-7
anaphoric repetition, 111
androgyny
    and Krull's character, 23, 25, 29-33, 40, 58, 61, 97, 105
    and primordial unity, 58
    and youthful beauty, 31
    in Greek art, 29
    of divinities, 29-33
    symbolism of, 29-30
    see also hermaphrodite figure, hermaphroditism
Andromache
    affinity with Krull, 64
    androgrynous character of, 61
    as female counterpart to Krull's androgyny, 61
    as heavenly goddess, 63, 66, 76
    as prefiguration of Senhora Kuckuck, 63
    as representation of hermaphrodite figure in Greek art, 61-62
    love precluded from her existence, 64, 67
    self-sufficient narcissism of, 64

GENERAL INDEX

symbolic function of, 63
anima, mother-daughter pair as projected image of, 76, 79
anthropological Darwinists, and cultural universals, 3
Aphrodite, *see* Hermes and Aphrodite
Aphroditos, 22
Apollo
    and Artemis, 47
    and Daphne, 93
    and Hermes, 12, 15, 108
    as symbol of objectivity and irony, 47
    as symbol of spiritual freedom and distance, 47
archetypal symbols, function of in Krull's development, 65-67
archetype
    dynamic effect of upon ego, 77
    form and content of, 66
    humanizing influence of, 65, 98
    Jungian characterization of, 50, 65
    reactivation and projection of, 64, 77
    superiority of over ego-consciousness, 77
    transpersonal nature of, 65
    see also Jung, Carl Gustav
Aristophanes, in Plato's *Symposium*, 94
arrow and lyre, meaning of for Thomas Mann, 108, 126, 141
    see also bow and lyre
Artemis
    as Apollo's twin-sister, 47
    as arouser of Hermes' sexuality, 24, 26, 48, 51
    Diane Philibert identified with, 46-54
    identified with Persephone, 27
    maternal solicitude of, 46, 50-51
    see also Diana, Philibert, Diane
Attic drama, Hermes' role in, 18
Attis, 32

Bastian, Adolf, 3
Bildungsroman, Krull's development as ironic reversal of, 1

bisexuality, *see* androgyny, hermaphrodite figure, hermaphroditism
Bloch, Adèle, 130
blood sacrifice
    motif of renewal in, 88, 91
    symbolism of, 84, 88, 90
    see also bull sacrifice
Blotner, Joseph L., 132
bow and lyre, kinship between, 108
    see also arrow and lyre
Brimo
    as arouser of Hermes' sexuality, 24
    identified with Artemis and Persephone, 24
    identified with Hecate, 47
Brinkmann, Hennig, *Die deutsche Sprache,* 141
brother-sister pair, 23, 26, 57-58, 61, 66, 77, 106, 125
Brown, Norman O., *Hermes the Thief,* 12-14
Bulfinch, Thomas, *The Age of Fable,* 55
bull sacrifice, symbolism of, 84, 88, 90, 91
    see also blood sacrifice

Campbell, Joseph, 131
Christ
    androgynous representation of in art, 32
    as second Adam, 32
Cicero
    De natura deorum, 23-24, 51
    description of arousal of Hermes' sexuality, 51
Cohen, J. M., 137
coincidentia oppositorum, as attribute of divinity, 33
collective unconscious, 65, 70, 92, 100
    as ultimate source of universality of psychic experience, 3
color symbolism, 83, 85
confessional memoir, *Felix Krull* as parody of, 1
contradictio in adjecto, 120-125
    see also oxymoron
cultural universals, 3

GENERAL INDEX

Curme, George O., *A Grammar of the German Language*, 141
Cybele, 32
    and Attis, 75-76

Delcourt, Marie, *Hermaphrodite*, 136, 137
Demeter, 24, 27
    as fertility goddess, 84
    seduced by Poseidon, 95
    Senhora Kuckuck as personification of, 80
Demeter-Persephone myth, 27, 71-73
    role of male as seducer in, 75
Diana
    and Endymion, 55
    as benefactress to farmers, 46
    as "friend of boys," 46
    as guardian of growing youth, 46
    as preserver and protectress, 46
    as virgin goddess of moon, 55
    identified with Artemis, 26, 46
    identified with Hecate, 47
    in search of male consort, 48
    maternal solicitude of, 46, 50-51, 55
    see also Artemis, Philibert, Diane
Dionysos, 32
double projection, 79

ego-libido, 44, 54, 92
    see also object-libido
Eleusis, 71
Eliade, Mircea
    on bisexuality of divinities, 32
    The Two and the One, 137
enantiodromia, 75
Endymion, 55
Enk, Petrus Johannes, 136
Eros, birth of, 23, 24
Eternal Feminine, and Jungian *anima*, 76
extraversion, in conflict with introversion, 37-38

GENERAL INDEX

father, archetypal role of, 90
Faust, and the journey to "The Mothers," 82
fertility ritual
    of Great Mother, 88
    role of nourishment in, 91
Fontane, Theodor, 109
    Effi Briest, 141
Frazer, Sir James George, 3
    The Golden Bough, 12, 48
Freud, Sigmund,
    and universality of psychic experience, 3, 5
    application of psychoanalysis to mythology and anthropology, 3
    on narcissism, 37-39, 44
    Totem and Taboo, 131

Gnosticism, 32
Goethe, Johann Wolfgang
    Wilhelm Meister, 1, 53
    see also Mignon
grammar, analogous to mythic pattern, 7-8
Great Mother
    color symbolism of, 83, 85
    identity of with bull, 84, 88
    mythological variants of, 75-76
    phallic symbols as attributes of, 84
    return to, 57
    Senhora Kuckuck as representation of, 75
    superiority of over ego-consciousness, 77, 83
    symbolic incest with, 96
Greek art
    and sexual dimorphism, 29
    representation of mother-daughter biunity in, 73
Greek myth, syncretism of, 47-48
Grimmelshausen, Hans Jakob Christoffel von, *Simplicissimus*, 1

Hadas, Moses, 135

GENERAL INDEX

Hecate
    and sexual crudity, 54
    as dark side of Artemis-Diana, 48
    as feminine counterpart to Apollo, 47
    identified with Artemis-Diana, 46-47
    identified with Brimo, 47
    identified with Persephone, 47
Heilman, Robert B., 129
Hemera, 24
Heraclitus
    and *enantiodromia*, 75
    on the bow and the lyre, 108
Hermaphrodite, *see* Hermaphroditus
hermaphrodite figure, 21-22
    as original state of Man, 94
    in art and ritual, 21-22, 63
    symbolism of, 21, 63
hermaphroditism
    as monstrosity to Ancients, 63
    distinguished from androgyny, 25-26
    see also androgyny
Hermaphroditus
    as symbol, 21
    origins of, 21, 25
Hermes
    adroitness of, 17-18
    and Aphrodite, 21-26, 52, 106
    and Apollo, 12, 15, 108
    and art of sly calculation, 15
    and art of verbal persuasion, 93
    as ceremonial minister, 18
    as consort of Aphrodite, 23
    as consort of Artemis-Diana, 23
    as cupbearer to gods, 18
    as "giver of joy," 16
    as god of unexpected gain, 55
    as guide to travelers, 12
    as herald, 18

as hermaphroditic, 22, 23
  as messenger and servant to Zeus, 18, 72
  as patron of commerce, 55
  as patron of servants, 17-18
  as patron of thieves, 12
  as *psychopompos*, 19
  descent of into underworld, 72
  friendliness of, 15
  guile of in verbal exchange, 15
  invention of lyre, 108
  role of in myth of Demeter and Persephone, 27
  separation of from bisexual fusion, 25, 52
  the magician, 13, 16
  the thief, 12, 13, 14, 18
  the traveler, 17
  the trickster, 12, 13, 15, 16, 18
  theft of Apollo's cattle, 12, 15
Hermes Trismegistus, 99
hermetics, 99
Hoffman, Frederick J., *Freudianism and the Literary Mind*, 130
Homeric Hymn to Demeter, 72, 94
homology, distinguished from analogy, 6-7
homosexuality, 25, 44
Houpflé, Madame, *see* Philibert, Diane
Hull, R. F. C., 137, 139

identity
  interchangeability of in mythology, 24, 28, 48
  interchangeability of in Krull, 28
  of father and son in myth, 25
individuality
  concept of in psychoanalysis, 4-5
  relativity of, 4-7
introversion, in conflict with extraversion, 37-38
irony, and dialectical tension, 114-120

Jacobson, Anna, 134

GENERAL INDEX

Jens, Walter, *Statt einer Literaturgeschichte*, 129
Jung, Carl Gustav
    and C. Kerenyi, *Essays on a Science of Mythology*, 132, 136, 138
    and universality of psychic experience, 3, 5
    application of psychoanalysis to mythology, 3
    definition of psychic wholeness, 65, 97
    interpretation of alchemical *conjunctio*, 100-105
    on variations of the mother archetype, 75
    psychic wholeness as goal of therapy, 65
    Symbols of Transformation, 139
    see also archetype

Kerenyi, Karl
    correspondence of with Thomas Mann, 4, 11, 71, 132, 134
    Das Ägyptische Fest, 71
    Das göttliche Kind, 132
    Hermes der Seelenführer, 12, 21, 136
    on the evocation of the male principle in Hermes, 23
    on the hermaphroditism of the primal Hermes, 22-23
    on the relation between Hermes and Aphrodite, 21-25
Koopmann, Helmut, *Die Entwicklung des intellektualen Romans bei Thomas Mann*, 129
Kris, Ernst, 5

libido, dynamics of in narcissism, 37-38, 40, 44
litotes, 119, 141
Logos, as paternal principle, 90
Loki, 32
Lowie, R. H., *The History of Ethnological Theory*, 131

magic
    and manipulation of external world, 17
    relation of to success at craftsmanship, 17
    relation of to trickery, 13
male principle
    evocation of, 23-27, 52

individuation of, 22, 106
Manheim, Ralph, 139
Mann, Thomas
    correspondence with Kerenyi, 4, 11, 71, 132, 134, 136
    intrest in myth, 20
    interest in psychoanalysis, 4
    on Hermes, 132-133
    on Jung, 132, 134
    on the individual versus the typical, 5-6
    on the relation of psychoanalysis to myth and creative literature, 3-4
    penchant for parody, 109-110
    preoccupation with idea of synthesis, 109
    treatment of myth, 27, 74-75, 92, 93, 94, 95
    works cited:
        "Bilse und Ich," 107-108, 141
        Death in Venice, 19, 20, 132
        "Der alte Fontane," 109
        Doktor Faustus, 109
        "Erziehung zur Sprache," 108-109
        "Freud und die Zukunft," 3-4, 130
        Joseph novels, 4, 5, 8, 10, 20, 31, 71, 82, 83, 105, 130, 133
        The Magic Mountain, 20, 99
        "Tischrede auf Pfitzner," 109
masochism, 54
matriarchy
    and Demeter-Persephone myth, 75, 85
    as characteristic of the Kuckuck family structure, 86
    role of male as seducer or conqueror in, 75, 87, 95
Mayor, Joseph B., 136
Mercurius
    as mediator, 102-103, 127
    as quicksilver, 103
    as symbol of union of opposites, 102-103, 127
    hermaphroditic nature of in alchemy, 103
Mignon, androgynous character of in *Wilhelm Meister*, 53
Mithraism, as patriarchal culture, 89

GENERAL INDEX

Mithras, 89
mother
    as beloved, 76
    as personification of the unconscious, 67, 76
mother archetype
    ambivalent nature of, 80, 83
    variants of in myth and religion, 75
mother and daughter, 27, 57, 66-67, 70
    biunity of, 24, 71, 73-74, 77, 79-80, 83, 91, 95, 96
    link with brother-sister pair, 70-71, 77
mother symbol
    Diane Philibert as, 77
    Senhora Kuckuck as, 76, 77
mythopoeic approach to literature
    frequent criticism against, 4
    underlying principles of, 6-9
    see also analogy, homology, psychoanalytic approach to literature

narcissism, 37-44, 58, 92
    and deflection from sexuality, 40-44
    and failure, 40
    and feeling of omnipotence, 39
    and infantile regression, 41
    and introversion, 38
    and success, 39
    as center of Krull's personality, 37
    connection with sleep, 38
    Freud's characterization of, 37-39, 44
    preconditions for reinforcement of, 39
    transference of, 39, 41, 60, 64
Neumann, Erich, 76, 77, 84, 87, 96, 97
Nicholas of Cusa, 33
Nicholson, Jennifer, 136

object-libido, 44, 54
    see also ego-libido, extraversion
Odin, 32

Odyssey, role of Hermes in, 18
Oedipus, victory of over Sphinx, 96
Otto, Walter F.
   Die Götter Griechenlands, 108, 134, 138
   on Hermes the traveler, 17
ouroboros, as alchemical symbol, 103
Ovid, *Metamorphoses*, 21
oxymoron, 107, 120-125

Persephone, 24, 27
   as arouser of Hermes' sexuality, 24, 51
   identified with Artemis, 27
   identified with Hecate, 47
   Zouzou identified with, 27
phallic symbols, as attributes of the Great Mother, 84
Philibert, Diane, 13-14, 19, 27, 45-54
   identified with Artemis-Diana, 26-27
   identifies Krull with Hermes, 13-14, 19, 45, 53
   love of for young boys, 50
   sexual perversion in, 54
Philosophers' Stone, 100, 103
Plato, *Symposium*, 94
Plöger, Jürgen, 129, 135
Pluto, abduction of Persephone, 27, 47, 72, 94
Poseidon, abduction of Demeter, 95
prima materia, hermaphroditic nature of in alchemy, 103, 104
projection, of *anima*, 76-77
Propertius, 24
prostitution, Krull as patron of, 36
psychoanalytic approach to literature, frequent criticism
   against, 4

qualification, as dominant trait of Mann's style, 113-120
quest motif, 48-49, 57, 91
quicksilver, alchemists' fascination with, 102
   see also Mercurius

GENERAL INDEX

rebirth, through re-entry into womb, 76, 91, 96-97
ritual killing, as transition to new fertility and rebirth, 91
   see also blood sacrifice, bull sacrifice
Roazen, Paul, *Freud: Political and Social Thought*, 131
Rousseau, Jean-Jacques, 1

Saint Augustine, 1
Salmacis, 21
Sappho, 18
Schiffer, Eva, 129, 142
Schneider, Wilhelm, *Stilistische deutsche Grammatik*, 141, 142
Seidlin, Oskar, 129, 141
separation, connection of with creation, 52
sex, differentiation of and separation, 51-52
sex drive, on origin of in Plato's *Symposium*, 94
sexual dimorphism, in Greek art, 29
Sheed, Rosemary, 137
Singer, Herbert, 141
sleep, connection with narcissism, 38
Socratic dialogue, connection with dialectic and irony, 114
Strachey, James, 131, 137
subordinate conjunction, role of in Mann's style, 114-120
syncretism, in myth, 47-48, 90

Terrible Mother, 80
theft
   and trickery, 13
   as manifestation of magical power, 13
traveling, as symbol of erotic longing, 49
trickery
   as manifestation of magical power, 13, 16
   relation of to technical skill, 16
trickster, as culture hero, 16
Tuisco, 32
Tylor, E. B., 3

unconscious
- as source of archetypal contents, 98
- as source of creativity, 97-98
- connection with myth, 66
- descent into, 69, 70, 81
- Senhora Kuckuck as personification of, 67

union of conscious and unconscious, 65, 90, 96, 106
union of opposites, bow and lyre as symbol of, 108
unity
- archetypal symbols of, 66
- longing for, 64-65, 67, 94, 106
- reactivation of primordial image of, 64, 77

unity in duality, 26, 58, 73, 90, 107
universal sympathy, 58
Uranos, 23

Vickery, John B., 132

Wiese, Benno von, 141
womb
- as symbol of unconscious, 38
- re-entry into and rebirth, 76, 91, 96-97

Yahweh, 33

Zeus, 18, 27, 72

www.ingramcontent.com/pod-product-compliance
Lightning Source LLC
Chambersburg PA
CBHW031314150426
43191CB00005B/225